COMPA TRAVEL GUIDE TO

KUSADISI, TURKEY

Must See, Must Do Activities! Top Attractions! insider and Local Tips! Cultural Immersion!

CARL DIAZ

COPYRIGHT NOTICE

This publication is copyright-protected. This is only for personal use. No part of this publication may be, reproduced, in any form or medium, stored in a data retrieval system or transmitted by or through any means, without prior written permission from the Author.

Legal action will be pursued if this is breached.

SCAN HERE TO GAIN ACCESS TO ALL MY BOOKS

DISCLAIMER

Please note that the information contained within this document is for educational purposes only. The information contained herein has been obtained from sources believed to be reliable at the time of publication. The opinions expressed herein are subject to change without notice. Readers acknowledge that the Author / Publisher is not engaging in rendering legal, financial or professional advice.

In addition, I disclaim all warranties as to the accuracy, completeness, or adequacy of such information. Also, note that the paperback is black and white, I understand that it is not ideal but so as to reduce cost; however, if you want a colored version, kindly check out the kindle version, it has full colored maps and images that you can zoom in, which is quite helpful.

Lastly, this guide is meant to give you all the basic info you need quickly, a shortcut to aid your planning without spending a lot of time online, so remember that this is just a starting point as there's always more to discover on your own. Thank you for choosing this city's guide, I hope it makes your journey memorable and easier.

Table of Contents

DISCLAIMER 3

WELCOME TO KUŞADASI 12

Introduction to Kuşadası 12

Brief History and Culture of Kuşadası 13

Cultural Heritage 15

Why visit Kuşadası? 18

Chapter 1 22

HOW TO GET THERE 22

By Air 22

Flights to Adnan Menderes Airport 23

From Adnan Menderes Airport to Kuşadası 24

Travel Tips for A Smooth Journey 27

Exploring İzmir En Route 28

By Sea 30

Cruise Ships 30

Ferries 32

Yachts and Private Boats 34

Additional Tips for Sea Travelers: 35

By Road 36

Driving to Kuşadası. 37

Scenic Stops and Attractions Along the Way: 39

Renting A Car: 40

Bus & Coach Services 41

Travel Tips for First-Time Visitors 43

Visa and Entry Requirements 45

    Visa Requirements 45

    Entry Requirements: 47

Chapter 2 52

BEST TIME TO VISIT 52

Weather Overview 52

Peak tourist seasons 53

Offseason Insights 54

Choosing the Right Time for You 55

Chapter 3 57

DURATION OF STAY 57

Ideal Length of Stay 57

    Short Stay (3-4 Days) 57

    Medium Stay (5-7 Days) 58

    Extended Stay (8-14 Days) 60

Suggested Stay Durations Based on Interests 62

    History Buffs 62

    Beach Lovers 63

    Adventure Seekers 64

    Cultural Enthusiasts 64

    Family Vacationers 65

    Wellness and Relaxation Seekers 65

Chapter 4 67

TOP TOURIST ATTRACTIONS IN KUŞADASI 67

Ephesus: Ancient Marvels 67

   Highlights of Ephesus 68

   Practical Tips for Visiting Ephesus 72

   Nearby Attractions 73

Güvercinada: The Pigeon Island 75

   The Fortress............ 76

   Scenic walks............ 77

   Marine Life & Snorkeling............ 78

   Picnicking and Relaxation............ 79

   Practical information............ 80

Kaleiçi Mosque: Historical Architecture 81

   Visiting Kaleiçi Mosque 82

   Nearby Attractions 83

   Practical Information............ 85

Dilek Peninsula National Park: Nature's Haven............ 85

   Highlights of Dilek Peninsula National Park 86

   Practical information............ 89

   Nearby Attractions 90

Adaland Aquapark: Family Fun............ 91

   Water Rides and Attractions 91

   Practical Information and Tips 95

   Nearby Attractions 96

Kusadasi Castle: Historical Fortification 96

Practical Information for Visitors 99

Highlights of Visiting Kusadasi Castle 100

Nearby Attractions 101

Chapter 5 103

HIDDEN GEMS AND LOCAL FAVORITES 103

Değirmen Yeri Mill: A Cozy Getaway 103

Highlights of Değirmen Yeri Mill 104

Tips for Visiting Değirmen Yeri Mill 108

Kirazlı Village: Traditional Turkish Charm 109

Exploring the Village: 110

Practical Tips for Visiting Kirazlı Village 115

Oleatrium: Olive and Olive Oil Museum 116

Museum highlights 116

Practical information 119

Pamucak Beach: Unwind in Serenity 121

Highlights of Pamucak Beach 122

Tips for visiting Pamucak Beach 124

Chapter 6 127

CULTURAL EXPERIENCES IN KUŞADASI, TURKEY 127

Turkish Cuisine: A Culinary Adventure 127

Traditional Markets and Bazaars 129

Local Festivals and Events 131

Ephesus Festival: A Celebration of History and
Culture 131

Selçuk Camel Wrestling Festival: A Unique Tradition 133

Local Music and Dance Performances: Feel the Rhythm 134

Religious Festivals: A Blend of Tradition and Spirituality 136

National Holidays: Celebrating Turkish Pride......... 137

Harvest Festivals: Celebrating Nature's Bounty..... 138

Annual Events and Celebrations 139

Tips for Attending Festivals and Events 141

Cultural Etiquette and Basic Phrases....................... 141

Chapter 7 145

ITINERARIES FOR EVERY TRAVELER 145

Three-Day Itinerary: Highlights of Kuşadası 145

Day 1: Exploring the Ancient Marvels 145

Day 2: Nature and Relaxation 146

Day 3: Cultural Immersion and Shopping 147

Seven-Day Itinerary: In-Depth Exploration 148

Day 1: Arrival and Orientation 148

Day 2: Ancient Wonders.. 149

Day 3: Nature and Adventure 150

Day 4: Cultural Exploration 151

Day 5: Beach and Leisure 151

Day 6: Shopping and Local Flavors........................ 152

Day 7: Relaxation and Departure 153

Family-Friendly Itinerary..................................... 154

    Day 1: Arrival and Family Orientation 154

    Day 2: Fun and Adventure.................................. 155

    Day 3: Educational and Entertaining..................... 155

Adventure Seeker's Itinerary 156

    Day 1: Arrival and Adventure Prep....................... 156

    Day 2: Hiking and Exploration 157

    Day 3: Water Adventures 158

Relaxation and Wellness Itinerary............................ 158

    Day 1: Arrival and Wellness Orientation 158

    Day 2: Spa and Relaxation 159

    Day 3: Beach and Leisure 160

Chapter 8.. 162

TRANSPORTATION WITHIN KUŞADASI 162

Public Transportation: Dolmuş and Buses.................. 162

    Using Dolmuş: 163

    Public buses:.. 164

Taxis and Car Rentals.. 165

    Taxis:... 165

    Car Rental: 167

Biking and Walking Routes 168

    Biking: 168

    Walking:... 169

Tips and Tricks for navigating the city 170

Chapter 9 174

ACCOMMODATION OPTIONS 174

Luxury Resorts and Hotels 174

Budget-friendly stays 176

Unique Accommodations: Boutique Hotels and
Guesthouses 178

Choosing the Right Accommodation for You 180

Booking Tips and Tricks 183

Booking Platforms 185

Chapter 10 189

DINING AND NIGHTLIFE IN KUŞADASI 189

Must-Try Restaurants 189

Street Food Delights 192

Best Spots for Nightlife and Entertainment 193

Wine Tasting and Local Brews 195

Chapter 11 198

SHOPPING IN KUŞADASI 198

Best Shopping Streets and Malls 198

Souvenirs to Take Home 200

Local Artisans & Crafts 202

Practical Tips for Shopping in Kuşadası 204

Chapter 12 206

WHAT TO DO AND NOT TO DO IN KUŞADASI 206

Important Dos and Don'ts for Tourists 206

Cultural Sensitivities and Respectful Behavior 209

Safety Tips and Common Scams to Avoid 210

Chapter 13 213

PRACTICAL INFORMATION 213

Currency and Money Exchange 213

Language & Communication 214

Health and Safety Tips 215

Staying connected 216

Navigating Public Services 217

Environmental Awareness 218

CONCLUSION 220

Final Tips for an Enjoyable Visit 220

Encouragement to Return and Explore More 220

APPENDIX: USEFUL RESOURCES 222

Emergency Contacts 222

Maps and Navigational Tools 223

Additional Reading and References 224

Useful Local Phrases 226

MAPS 229

WELCOME TO KUŞADASI

Welcome to the breathtaking coastal town of Kuşadası! Nestled on Turkey's Aegean coast, this bustling and historic town is the starting point for a plethora of excursions. Allow me to take you on a tour of its beauty, from ancient ruins to sun-kissed beaches, and all in between. Kuşadası offers unique experiences for both first-time visitors and seasoned travelers alike.

Introduction to Kuşadası

Kuşadası, which translates to "Bird Island," is a picturesque town known for its stunning coastal views, historical significance, and warm, inviting atmosphere. The town's history extends back to antiquity, with influences from the Greeks, Romans, and Ottomans establishing its own cultural legacy. Today, Kuşadası is a popular tourist site that combines modern comforts with its rich history.

Kuşadası's streets offer a unique blend of old and new, sure to enchant visitors. The town center is a wonderful blend of traditional markets, modern boutiques, and delightful cafés. The dynamic harbor area is the town's core, with a lively promenade lined with restaurants, cafes, and stores, as well as spectacular views of the Aegean Sea.

Brief History and Culture of Kuşadası

Kuşadası is more than a gorgeous coastal town; it's a rich tapestry of history and culture that captivates visitors. Walking through its streets takes you through millennia of history, from ancient civilizations to the bustling modern-day town you see today. Join me as I explore Kuşadası's rich history and culture.

Ancient beginnings

Kuşadası has a long history, with settlements dating back to 3000 BCE. The Leleges and Carians, ancient Anatolian peoples, were the first to settle in the region. Kuşadası's strategic location on the Aegean coast made it an important port and commerce center.

The town was later colonized by the Ionians, who established the nearby city of Neapolis. However, it was during the Hellenistic period that the area began to thrive. Ephesus, located near Kuşadası, was a significant city in ancient Greek culture. It was known for its majestic architecture, bustling waterfront, and as a hub of learning and culture.

The Roman era

In 129 BCE, Ephesus and the surrounding territory, including Kuşadası, fell under Roman authority. This period marked a time of prosperity and growth. Ephesus became the seat of the Roman province of Asia, and its population grew to more than 250,000, making it one of the biggest towns in antiquity.

The Romans made a lasting impression on the region, constructing great facilities such as the Library of Celsus, the Great Theatre, and the Temple of Artemis, one of the Seven Wonders of the Ancient World. Roman culture, architecture, and infrastructure had a significant impact on Kuşadası, a major port at the period.

Byzantine and Ottoman Influence

With the decline of the Roman Empire, Kuşadası and Ephesus fell under Byzantine rule. Fortifications and churches were built throughout the Byzantine period, and some of them can still be found today. During the Ottoman period, Kuşadası evolved into its current shape.

In the early 15th century, Kuşadası became part of the Ottoman Empire. The Ottomans recognized the town's strategic importance and invested in its growth. They built the city walls, the famous Kaleiçi Mosque, and the Kusadasi Castle, which still dominates the town's skyline.

Modern era

The 20th century marked considerable changes in Kuşadası. The town underwent fast expansion and development, evolving from a sleepy fishing village to a thriving tourist destination. The development of contemporary services, hotels, and infrastructure attracted people from all over the world, lured by the town's rich history, stunning beaches, and dynamic culture.

Today, Kuşadası is a prosperous town that integrates its old past with modern amenities. The town's ancient sites are well-preserved and provide an insight into its rich history, while its bustling harbor, markets, and cultural festivals reflect its modern character.

Cultural Heritage

Kuşadası's culture reflects the region's unique history and influences from other civilizations. The town's cultural legacy is reflected in its architecture, food, traditions, and festivals.

Architecture

The architecture of Kuşadası is a testament to its rich history. Walking through the town, you'll see a variety of styles, including old ruins, Ottoman-era buildings, and modern constructions. The Kaleiçi Mosque, with its unique minaret and elaborate tilework, is a stunning specimen of Ottoman architecture.

Kusadasi Castle, perched on Pigeon Island, offers panoramic views of the town and the Aegean Sea. The castle's walls and towers serve as a reminder of the town's strategic importance and role in safeguarding the coastline.

Cuisine

Turkish cuisine is known for its various flavors and inspirations, and Kuşadası is no exception. The town's culinary culture is a beautiful combination of traditional Turkish meals and fresh seafood, reflecting its coastal position.

Don't pass up the opportunity to try kebabs, mezes (small appetizers), and baklava. Local markets are sensory delights, offering fresh food, spices, and handcrafted goodies. Kuşadası restaurants have breathtaking sea views and a welcoming atmosphere, making dining an unforgettable experience.

Traditions and Festivals

Kuşadası proudly celebrates its culture and heritage. Throughout the year, the town conducts a number of festivals and events to celebrate its traditions, music, and dancing. The International Kuşadası Golden Pigeon Music Festival showcases the town's artistic vitality and draws performers from all over the world.

Kuşadası values traditional Turkish music and dance as part of its cultural identity. You might get the opportunity to see a lively folk dance performance or listen to the haunting sounds of classic instruments such as the saz and the oud.

Markets and bazaars

Kuşadası's markets and bazaars offer a rich cultural experience. The Grand Bazaar, located in the town center, is a maze of stores that sell everything from handcrafted crafts and textiles to jewelry and souvenirs. It's the ideal spot to collect one-of-a-kind souvenirs from your trip.

To get a more real experience, head to the weekly market, where locals buy fresh produce, spices, and household items. This is a great opportunity to meet locals and experience daily life in Kuşadası.

Why visit Kuşadası?

What makes Kuşadası such a popular tourist destination? Okay, let me tell you! This charming town provides a variety of experiences for all types of travelers. Kuşadası caters to a wide range of interests, including history, beach, adventure, and relaxation.

Rich History and Culture

Kuşadası is a must-see destination for history buffs. The surrounding ancient city of Ephesus is a UNESCO World Heritage Site and one of the most well-preserved classical cities in the Mediterranean. Walking through Ephesus' marble streets, one can almost hear the echoes of its past, from the enormous Library of Celsus to the magnificent Great Theatre.

Kuşadası has various historical attractions, notably the Ottoman-era Kaleiçi Mosque and the impressive Kusadasi Castle. These landmarks provide a look into the town's rich history and demonstrate its cultural relevance.

Stunning natural beauty

Kuşadası is a nature lover's heaven. The town is surrounded by breathtaking scenery, ranging from the lush vegetation of Dilek Peninsula National Park to the golden sands of its gorgeous beaches. Ladies Beach, with its crystal-clear seas and lively environment, is popular with both locals and tourists.

Pamucak Beach, a secluded refuge away from the masses, is ideal for those wanting a more relaxing escape. The blue waves of the Aegean Sea create an ideal setting for relaxation and restoration.

Vibrant Local Life

Kuşadası is known for its active local life. The town's markets and bazaars are sensory delights, allowing you to immerse yourself in the sights, sounds, and scents of Turkish culture. The markets, which sell everything from fresh fruit to homemade goods, provide a look into the inhabitants' daily lives.

Kuşadası's locals welcome visitors with warmth and hospitality. Engaging with people and seeing their way of life personalizes your experience, making it genuinely unforgettable.

Diverse activities and experiences

Whether you're an adrenaline junkie or someone who prefers a leisurely pace, Kuşadası has a wide range of activities to suit your preferences. Water sports enthusiasts can participate in activities such as diving, snorkeling, and windsurfing, while those seeking a more relaxing experience can take a leisurely boat cruise along the coastline.

Kuşadası offers a variety of excursions, such as visiting adjacent islands, cultural tours, and hiking. The town's strategic location gives it an ideal starting point for exploring the surrounding areas and discovering hidden gems.

Culinary delights

Let us not forget the food! Turkish food, including Kuşadası, is well-known for its rich flavors and variety. The town's culinary scene is a feast for the senses, with classic kebabs and mezes with fresh fish and wonderful sweets.

Kuşadası restaurants have breathtaking sea views and a welcoming atmosphere, making dining an unforgettable experience. Kuşadası offers a variety of dining options, including waterfront restaurants and neighborhood cafés, that will leave you wanting more.

Embrace the Journey

Kuşadası offers a variety of experiences and lasting memories. Kuşadası celebrates the basic pleasures of life, whether it's exploring historical ruins, relaxing on sun-drenched beaches, or learning about local culture.

So, pack your bags, set your sights on this charming town, and prepare to embark on a journey that will captivate both your heart and mind. Kuşadası combines history, nature, and culture to offer a genuinely spectacular experience.

Chapter 1

HOW TO GET THERE

As someone who has spent significant time exploring the charming beach village of Kuşadası, Turkey, I'm pleased to share my experiences and thoughts on how to go to this beautiful area. Whether you arrive by plane, sea, or road, there are several options to fit your travel needs. Let's dive into the specifics to ensure your journey to Kuşadası is as smooth and enjoyable as possible.

By Air

Traveling to Kuşadası by air is a popular choice, especially for international visitors and those coming from other parts of Turkey. Kuşadası does not have an airport, so the most convenient choice is Adnan Menderes Airport (ADB) in İzmir. This airport provides convenient connectivity to major cities in Europe, the Middle East, and Turkey, making it an ideal starting point for your Kuşadası excursion.

Flights to Adnan Menderes Airport

- **International Flights:** Adnan Menderes Airport is served by numerous international airlines, making it easy to find direct flights from various European and Middle Eastern cities. Turkish Airlines, Lufthansa, British Airways, and Air France offer regular flights to İzmir. Budget airlines like Pegasus Airlines and easyJet also provide low flights from several European destinations.
- **Domestic Flights:** If you're already in Turkey, you can catch a domestic flight to İzmir from major cities like Istanbul, Ankara, Antalya, and Bodrum. Domestic carriers like Turkish Airlines, Pegasus Airlines, and SunExpress provide regular flights, giving you more flexibility in your travel plans. Flights from Istanbul to İzmir are accessible many times a day and take approximately an hour.

Booking Tips:

- **Advance Booking:** To secure the best deals, book your flight well in advance, especially if you're traveling during the peak tourist season (June to September).

- **Flexible dates:** If you have flexible travel dates, try fare comparison tools such as Skyscanner or Google Flights to locate the cheapest days to fly.
- **Baggage Allowance:** Check your airline's baggage limitation, especially if you're flying with a low-cost carrier, as they typically have tougher limits and additional taxes for checked bags.

From Adnan Menderes Airport to Kuşadası.

Upon arrival at Adnan Menderes Airport, various options for transportation are available to reach Kuşadası, tailored to individual tastes and budget. Let's go over these possibilities in detail:

Private Transfer:

A private transfer provides the most pleasant and hassle-free experience. Here's what you should know.

- **Booking:** You can reserve a private transfer online in advance through services such as Welcome Pickups, Shuttle Direct, or directly with your hotel if they provide this service.
- **Cost:** A private transfer costs between €50 and €80, depending on the vehicle type and number of passengers. It's worth paying the extra money

for the convenience, especially if you're traveling with family or a group.

- **Journey Time:** The drive from the airport to Kuşadası takes approximately 1.5 hours, depending on traffic. The driver will follow the most efficient route, so you can relax and enjoy the scenery.

Shuttle Service:

Shuttle services offer a cost-effective alternative to private transports, with shared rides between the airport and Kuşadası.

- **Booking:** You can make a shuttle reservation online or at the airport upon arrival. Companies such as Havas and Ephesus Shuttle provide regular services.
- **Cost**: The cost for a shuttle service is typically between €15 and €25 per person.
- **Journey Time:** The travel time is identical to that of a private transfer, but allow extra time for picking up and dropping off other passengers.

Car Rental:

Renting a car allows you to explore Kuşadası and the neighboring areas at your own time. Here are some tips for renting a car:

- **Rental Companies:** Adnan Menderes Airport hosts desks for major international rental companies such as Avis, Hertz, and Europcar, as well as local companies.

- **Booking:** It is recommended that you book your car hire in advance to get the best pricing and ensure availability, especially during peak seasons.
- **Driving in Turkey:** Driving in Turkey is relatively straightforward, but it's important to familiarize yourself with local traffic laws and regulations. The attractive and enjoyable travel to Kuşadası is made possible by well-maintained roads.
- **Cost:** Car rental prices vary, but you can expect to pay around €25-€40 per day for a standard car. Remember to factor in the cost of petrol and any additional insurance coverage you may require.

Public Bus:

For budget-conscious tourists, taking a public bus is the most cost-effective choice, however it needs a little more work.

- **Step 1:** Shuttle or Taxi to İzmir Bus Terminal: First, you'll need to get from the airport to the İzmir bus terminal (Otogar). You can take the Havas shuttle, which runs often and costs roughly €5, or a taxi, which costs between €15 and €20.

- **Step 2:** Bus to Kuşadası: From the bus terminal, various bus companies offer trips to Kuşadası. Search for companies such as Pamukkale and Kamil Koç. The bus travel takes approximately 2 hours and costs around €10.
- **Tickets:** Bus tickets can be purchased at the terminal or online via the bus company's website.

Travel Tips for A Smooth Journey

- **Airport Facilities:** Adnan Menderes Airport provides a variety of amenities to provide a relaxing start to your journey. These include currency exchange facilities, ATMs, free Wi-Fi, a variety of food options, and duty-free shopping. If you want to unwind before continuing your journey, there are lounges accessible.
- **Luggage Services:** If you have a long layover or wish to explore İzmir briefly before heading to Kuşadası, the airport provides luggage storage services where you can securely leave your bags.
- **Customs and Immigration:** As with any overseas trip, be sure you have the appropriate travel documentation, such as a valid passport and visa (if applicable). Turkey has an e-Visa

service for several nationalities, which can be applied for online before your travel.

- **Local SIM Card:** Maintaining connectivity is critical, particularly for navigation and communication. Consider buying a local SIM card at the airport. Turkcell, Vodafone, and Türk Telekom provide kiosks in the arrivals terminal where you can purchase SIM cards and data packages.
- **Airport Assistance:** Adnan Menderes Airport offers wheelchair assistance and priority boarding to those with special requirements or who require assistance. It is recommended that you tell your airline in advance if you require any special accommodations.
- **Currency Exchange:** While it's a good idea to have some local currency on hand, avoid exchanging big sums at the airport because the rates are usually less advantageous. To get better rates, withdraw cash from ATMs or exchange it at local banks or exchange offices in Kuşadası.

Exploring İzmir En Route

Spend some time touring İzmir before heading to Kuşadası. İzmir is a dynamic city with a rich history, breathtaking seaside vistas, and bustling markets. Here are some highlights:

- **Konak Square:** Visit the iconic İzmir Clock Tower, a symbol of the city, located in Konak Square. The area also houses the popular Kemeraltı Bazaar, where visitors may shop for souvenirs, spices, and local handicrafts.
- **Alsancak:** This lively region is noted for its boisterous nightlife, fashionable eateries, and stunning coastal promenade. It's an excellent place to unwind and appreciate the city's vibe.
- **Kadifekale:** Explore the ancient ruins of Kadifekale (Velvet Castle), which offers panoramic views of the city and the Gulf of İzmir. It's an excellent destination for history buffs and photographers.
- **Ephesus Museum:** If you're interested in history, the Ephesus Museum in İzmir houses a fascinating collection of artifacts from the nearby ancient city of Ephesus, giving you a glimpse into the region's rich past.
- **Transportation to Kuşadası:** After your brief exploration, you can easily continue your journey to Kuşadası by catching a bus or shuttle from the city center to the bus terminal.

By Sea

Traveling to Kuşadası by sea provides a thrilling and spectacular view of the gorgeous Aegean coastline. Whether you're visiting on a large Mediterranean cruise or a local ferry from the adjacent Greek islands, docking in this picturesque town will leave you with wonderful memories. Here are the specifics to assist you plan your maritime travel to Kuşadası.

Cruise Ships

Kuşadası is a famous port for Mediterranean cruises due to its strategic location and proximity to the ancient city of Ephesus. Cruise lines including Royal Caribbean, Norwegian Cruise Line, MSC Cruises, and Celebrity Cruises frequently include Kuşadası on their itineraries. Here's everything you need to know if you're arriving by cruise ship:

1. Port Facilities: The Port of Kuşadası offers excellent facilities to accommodate cruise passengers. Upon arrival, you'll discover a well-organized terminal with customs and immigration services, currency exchange, and information kiosks to help you get about town. There are various stores, cafes, and restaurants in the port area where you may unwind before or after your excursions.

2. Shore Excursions: Many cruise lines offer organized shore excursions that allow you to explore the highlights of Kuşadası and its surroundings. Popular excursions include guided tours of Ephesus, the House of the Virgin Mary, and the Temple of Artemis. These excursions are convenient because they include transportation and skilled guides, so you won't miss any significant sights.

3. Independent Exploration: Kuşadası's harbor is easily accessible from the town center, making it ideal for solo exploration. You may simply walk to crowded markets, quaint cafes, and historical landmarks. For those seeking to explore further, cabs and local tour companies are easily accessible at the port, allowing you to choose your own route.

4. Tip for Cruise Passengers:

- **Timing:** Keep track of the time your ship is docked and organize your activities accordingly. Allow sufficient time to return to the ship before departing.
- **Currency:** While many shops in Kuşadası accept major credit cards, having some Turkish Lira for modest transactions and tips is recommended.

- **Safety:** While Kuşadası is generally safe for tourists, it's important to be cautious of your surroundings and safeguard your things.

Ferries

For travelers coming from nearby Greek islands, taking a ferry to Kuşadası is a convenient and picturesque option. Samos offers frequent boat connections to Kuşadası, making it ideal for island hopping and exploring multiple places.

1. Ferry routes:

- **Samos to Kuşadası:** The ferry rides from Samos to Kuşadası takes approximately 90 minutes, offering beautiful views of the Aegean Sea. Ferries depart from Vathy or Pythagorio on Samos, arriving at the major port in Kuşadası.
- **Other Greek Islands:** While Samos is the most popular starting point, there are infrequent ferry connections from nearby islands such as Chios. Check local ferry schedules, as they may vary seasonally.

2. Book Your Ferry:

- **Advance Booking:** It is recommended that you reserve your ferry tickets in advance, particularly during peak tourist seasons (June to September). Tickets can be booked online through numerous ferry companies or purchased at the pier.

- **Ticket Options:** Ferries provide various types of tickets, ranging from regular seating to more luxurious lounge sections. Choose based on your budget and comfort preferences.

3. Arrival in Kuşadası:

- **Customs and Immigration:** Upon landing at Kuşadası, you will go through these procedures. Make sure you have your passport and any other travel paperwork handy. The procedure is usually simple and efficient.
- **Port Location:** The ferry terminal is strategically positioned, providing convenient access to the town's attractions. From the dock, you can walk to surrounding attractions or take a taxi to your hotel or other destination.

4. Tips for Ferry Travelers:

- **Travel Light:** Ferries can get crowded, so bringing lightweight and compact luggage makes the trip more enjoyable.
- **Seasickness:** If you are prone to seasickness, consider taking medication before your trip, as the sea can be turbulent at times.

- **Onboard Facilities:** Most boats include basic amenities such as bathrooms and food bars. Bring some snacks and drink on the trip.

Yachts and Private Boats

Arriving at Kuşadası by yacht or private boat offers an exceptional and personalized experience. The town's marina accommodates private vessels and provides a variety of services and amenities.

1. Kuşadası Setur Marina.

- **Facilities:** Kuşadası Setur Marina is a modern and well-equipped facility, providing berths for yachts of various sizes. The marina has water and electrical hookups, fuel services, and 24-hour security.
- **Services:** Additional services include laundry facilities, Wi-Fi, and maintenance services. The marina complex also has multiple restaurants, bars, and shops, so you'll have all you need for a great stay.
- **Booking a Berth**: It is suggested that you reserve your space in advance, especially during the summer months when the marina is busiest. You can make bookings online or call the marina directly.

2. Sail to Kuşadası:

- **Navigation:** If you're sailing your own boat, be sure you have current nautical charts and are familiar with local maritime regulations. The approach to Kuşadası is simple, however it's important to verify weather conditions and maritime advisories.
- **Clearance Procedures:** Upon arrival, you must pass customs and immigration clearance. The marina's personnel can help you with the relevant paperwork and procedures.

3. Exploring by Boat:

- **Day Trips and Excursions:** Having your own boat allows you to explore the lovely coastline and surrounding islands. Popular day outings include exploring the Dilek Peninsula's quiet coves and beaches, as well as sailing to adjacent Greek islands.
- **Fishing and Diving:** The waters around Kuşadası are rich in marine life, making it a great spot for fishing and diving. Several diving schools and charter services offer equipment and advice for underwater expeditions.

Additional Tips for Sea Travelers:

- **Check the weather:** The Aegean Sea is unpredictable, so always check the weather prediction before setting out. Windy winds can disrupt boat schedules and make the sea rough.
- **Stay informed:** Keep an eye out for local marine alerts and announcements, especially if you're traveling during the off-season, when ferry service may be less regular.
- **Travel Insurance:** Make sure your policy covers maritime travel. This is especially vital if you're chartering a boat or participating in aquatic activities.
- **Health precautions:** If you are prone to seasickness, bring motion sickness medicine or natural cures such as ginger candies. Staying hydrated and avoiding big meals before the flight can also be beneficial.
- **Respect Local Regulations:** When docking and mooring in Kuşadası, adhere to local maritime regulations and guidelines. Respect the environment by not mooring in protected areas and disposing of rubbish properly.

By Road

Traveling to Kuşadası by car offers a handy way to explore Turkey's beautiful landscapes and cultural heritage. Whether you drive yourself or take the bus, the journey will be part of the adventure. Here's a detailed guide for driving to Kuşadası.

Driving to Kuşadası.

Driving to Kuşadası offers the flexibility to explore at your own pace and make impromptu stops along the way. Here are some important aspects to consider:

Routes and highways:

From Istanbul:

- The most typical route is along the O-5 and D550/E87 roads.
- Begin on the O-5 highway, a contemporary toll route that leads south towards Bursa.
- Continue on the O-5 after crossing Bursa until it connects with the D550/E87 highway near Balıkesir.
- Follow the D550/E87 south past Manisa until you reach İzmir.
- From İzmir, take the D550/E87 southeast directly to Kuşadası.

- The overall driving distance is around 600 kilometers (370 miles), and the trip usually takes six to seven hours, depending on traffic and road conditions.

From İzmir:

- Take D550/E87 highway southeast to Kuşadası.
- This is a straightforward drive of about 80 kilometers (50 miles) and typically takes around an hour and a half.

From Ankara:

- Continue west on the O-4 highway, which joins with the D200/E90 highway around Eskişehir.
- Continue along the D200/E90 via Kütahya until you reach the D550/E87 highway near Uşak.
- Follow the D550/E87 south to İzmir, then southeast to Kuşadası.
- The overall route is around 650 kilometers (400 miles), and the ride often takes eight hours.

Road Conditions and Driving Tips:

- **Toll roads:** Turkey boasts a well-kept network of toll roads. Make sure you have an HGS or OGS toll payment sticker for your vehicle. These can be obtained at post offices, certain banks, and some gas stations.
- **Rest sites:** There are various rest sites along the highways that provide clean restrooms, eateries,

and gas stations. They are perfect for taking a break and renewing oneself along the way.

- **Navigation:** GPS navigation systems are effective in Turkey. Google Maps and other navigation apps provide accurate routes and real-time traffic updates. Make sure your phone is completely charged, and consider taking a car charger.
- **Driving Etiquette:** Turkish drivers can be assertive, especially in larger cities. Always wear your seatbelt, follow the speed limit, and be prepared for rapid lane changes by other drivers.

Scenic Stops and Attractions Along the Way:

From Istanbul:

- **Bursa:** Known for its historical sites and thermal baths. The city is well known for the Mount Uludağ ski resort.
- **Balıkesir:** A great place to sample local cheeses and olive oil. The town itself boasts attractive streets and a laidback vibe.
- **İzmir:** Visit this vibrant seaside city to discover its bustling markets, oceanfront promenade, and historic sites like the Agora.

From Ankara:

- Eskişehir is a city recognized for its youthful atmosphere, especially to its universities. Explore the Odunpazarı district and its traditional Ottoman houses.
- **Kütahya:** Famous for its ceramics and tiles. The village boasts stunning Ottoman architecture and various pottery workshops.
- **Uşak:** Home to historical sites and natural beauty, including the Ulubey Canyon, which is one of the longest in the world.

Renting A Car:

Renting a car is a convenient option if you prefer to drive. Here's what you should know.

- **Rental Agencies:** Major international car rental businesses such as Avis, Hertz, and Europcar operate in Turkey, as do reputable local agencies.
- **Requirements:** A valid driver's license is required while renting an automobile. An international driving permit (IDP) is encouraged but not necessarily required. You must also have a credit card to pay the security deposit.

- **Insurance:** Make sure your rental includes full insurance. It's also a good idea to verify whether your travel insurance covers automobile rentals.
- **Cost:** Rental fees vary according on the type of vehicle and the length of the rental. Booking in advance usually results in a better deal.
- **Parking:** In Kuşadası, parking can be challenging during peak tourist season. Many hotels provide parking, and there are public parking lots accessible.

Bus & Coach Services

Traveling to Kuşadası by bus or coach is both affordable and comfortable. Turkey's intercity bus network is large, with contemporary coaches that have facilities to make your ride more comfortable.

Major Bus Companies:

- **Pamukkale:** One of Turkey's biggest and most dependable bus companies. Their coaches are pleasant, with reclining seats, air conditioning, and on-board snacks.
- **Kamil Koç:** Another popular alternative, recognized for its large network and high-quality service. Buses are equipped with Wi-Fi, entertainment systems, and food.

- **Metro Turizm:** Offers numerous routes across Turkey, including several daily services to Kuşadası. Their coaches are well-maintained and offer excellent service.

Booking tickets:

- **Online:** You can purchase tickets via the bus company's website or through popular Turkish travel applications such as Obilet and Busbud.
- Tickets are available for purchase at the bus terminal (otogar) in your departure city. Booking in advance is a wise idea, especially during high travel seasons.

Comfort and Amenities:

- **Seats:** Most long-distance buses include comfy, reclining seats with plenty of legroom.
- **Facilities:** Buses are equipped with air conditioning, Wi-Fi, power outlets, and personal entertainment screens.
- **Refreshments:** Onboard attendants provide complimentary drinks and snacks. Some buses also make stops at rest spots where passengers can purchase meals.
- **Luggage:** There is normally no additional price for luggage. Each passenger has a considerable luggage allowance, which includes storage space in the bus's cargo hold and overhead compartments for smaller bags.

Scenic routes:

- From Istanbul, you'll travel through the magnificent Marmara region, which features rolling hills and lovely villages. As you near İzmir, the terrain becomes more rough, with spectacular mountains and rich foliage.
- The path from İzmir to Kuşadası passes through the rich plains of the Aegean area. You'll pass vineyards, olive orchards, and quaint rural communities.

Tips for Bus Travel:

- **Book in advance:** Buses often fill up rapidly, especially during peak hours. Booking in advance guarantees you a seat on your selected departure.
- **Pack Essentials:** Bring a small travel pillow, a blanket or shawl, headphones, and snacks to make your trip more comfortable.
- **Rest stations:** Use the rest stations to stretch your legs, use the restroom, and get additional refreshments if necessary.

Travel Tips for First-Time Visitors

- **Plan Your Route in Advance:** Whether you're flying, sailing, or driving, preplanning your itinerary can save you time and stress. Book your tickets and transfers ahead of time, and have a backup plan in case of unforeseen changes.
- **Travel Light:** Kuşadası's lovely streets and sights are best enjoyed without carrying large bags. Pack lightweight, comfortable clothing appropriate for the Mediterranean temperature, and don't forget sunscreen, a hat, and comfortable walking shoes.
- **Stay Connected:** Having a reliable mode of communication is essential, especially if you are traveling alone. To stay connected, consider obtaining either a local SIM card or an international roaming plan.
- **Local Currency:** The local currency in Turkey is the Turkish Lira (TRY). It is a good idea to keep some cash on hand for modest purchases, especially if you are going by bus or taxi. ATMs are widely distributed, and credit cards are accepted in most places.
- **Language:** While English is widely spoken in tourist regions, learning a few basic Turkish phrases can improve your travel experience and allow you to engage with people.
- **Travel Insurance:** Make sure you have adequate travel insurance that covers medical

expenditures, trip cancellations, and other unforeseen concerns. It's best to be cautious than sorry, especially when traveling internationally.

- **Respect Local Customs:** Given Turkey's rich cultural legacy, it is critical to respect local customs and traditions. Dress modestly when visiting religious locations, and always get permission before photographing individuals.

Visa and Entry Requirements

To plan a hassle-free trip to Kuşadası, Turkey, it's important to understand the visa and entry procedures. Here's a complete guide based on my experience and the most recent information.

Visa Requirements

For EU, UK, and US Citizens:

- **Tourist Visa:** Citizens of numerous European Union nations, the United Kingdom, and the United States are not need to obtain a visa to visit Turkey for up to 90 days within a 180-day period.

This is part of Turkey's visa waiver arrangement with these nations.

- **E-Visa:** Turkey provides an electronic visa (e-Visa) application facility for individuals in need of one. You can apply for an e-Visa online prior to your travel. The procedure is basic and usually takes only a few minutes to finish.
- **Application:** Go to the official Republic of Turkey e-Visa website.
- **Requirements:** You will need a valid passport, an email address, and a credit or debit card to pay the visa fee.
- **Duration:** The e-Visa allows for multiple entries and is valid for stays of up to 90 days within 180 days.
- **Processing Time:** Most e-Visas are approved within 24 hours, although it is best to apply at least 48 hours before your travel date.

For Canadian, Australian, and New Zealand citizens:

- **Visa-Free Entry:** Citizens of Canada, Australia, and New Zealand may enter Turkey without a visa for stays of up to 90 days during a 180-day period.

For other nationalities:

- **Visa on Arrival**: Some nationalities are eligible for a visa on arrival, but it is always advisable to verify the most recent restrictions before traveling. Visa on arrival is available at major Turkish airports, including Adnan Menderes Airport in İzmir.

- **E-Visa:** Many other nationalities can apply for an e-Visa online. Visit the official Republic of Turkey e-Visa website to learn more about the eligibility requirements.
- **Traditional Visa:** If your nation is not qualified for visa-free entry or an e-Visa, you must apply for a visa at the Turkish consulate or embassy in your home country. Additional documents may be required, including a visa application form, a valid passport, passport-sized pictures, proof of accommodation, a travel itinerary, and proof of financial means.

Schengen Visa Holders:

- **No Special Privileges:** Holding a Schengen visa does not grant any special entry privileges to Turkey. You must meet the Turkish visa requirements pertaining to your nationality.

Entry Requirements:

Passport validity:

- Your passport must be valid for at least six months after your intended departure from Turkey.
- Ensure that your passport contains at least one blank page for entry and departure stamps.

Health and Vaccination Requirements:

- **Routine Vaccinations:** It's advisable to be up-to-date on routine vaccines before traveling to Turkey. These include MMR (measles, mumps, rubella), diphtheria-tetanus-pertussis, varicella (chickenpox), polio, and your yearly flu shot.
- **Recommended Vaccinations:** Depending on your travel goals and personal health, immunizations against hepatitis A and B, typhoid, and rabies may be suggested. For personalized advice, consult with your healthcare physician.
- **COVID-19 Measures:** Due to the ongoing global situation, travelers may be required to provide proof of COVID-19 immunization or a negative PCR test result obtained within 72 hours of departure. Check the most recent guidelines from both your own country and Turkish authorities, as these are subject to change.

Entry Procedures at the Border:

- Upon arrival in Turkey, you'll go through immigration control where an officer will check your passport and visa (if applicable).
- Prepare to answer a few typical questions regarding the purpose of your visit and your lodging arrangements.
- Make sure you have copies of your airline itinerary, hotel reservations, and trip insurance, since they may be needed.

Customs regulations:

- **Currency:** There is no limit to the amount of international or Turkish currency you can bring into the country. However, if you have more than 10,000 Euros (or equivalent), you must declare it upon arrival.
- **Duty-free Allowance:** You are permitted to bring in a fair number of personal things, such as clothing and electrical equipment. In addition, duty-free allowances include up to 600 cigarettes, 100 cigarillos, 50 cigars, or 250 grams of tobacco, and up to 2 liters of alcoholic beverages.
- **Prohibited Items:** Importing drugs, weapons, and certain items of cultural or historical significance without proper authorization is strictly prohibited. If you're unclear about something, check with Turkish customs before your travel.

Travel insurance:

Comprehensive travel insurance is generally recommended, as it covers medical emergencies, trip cancellations, lost luggage, and other potential concerns. Ensure that your policy covers the activities you intend to do in Turkey.

Local Law and Etiquette:

- **Respect for Local Customs:** Turkey is largely Muslim, with a rich cultural heritage. Dress modestly, especially while visiting religious sites, and respect local customs and traditions.
- **Legal Drinking Age**: The legal drinking age in Turkey is 18. Drinking alcohol in public areas (excluding licensed establishments) is generally prohibited.
- **Drug Laws:** Turkey has strict drug laws, and penalties for possession, use, or trafficking of illegal drugs are severe. Always follow local laws and avoid getting involved with illegal substances.

Practical Tips for a Smooth Entry

- **Check for Updates:** Visa and entry criteria are subject to change, so always check the latest information from official sources before your travel.

- **Print Copies:** Have printed copies of your e-Visa, travel insurance, hotel reservations, and airline information. While digital copies are usually sufficient, hardcopy documents can be useful in the event of technical difficulties.
- **Stay informed:** Keep an eye on your own country's travel advisories, particularly for health and safety concerns.
- **Be patient:** Immigration lines can be long, especially during high travel seasons. Patience and a pleasant manner will go a long way.

To ensure a smooth start to your Kuşadası vacation, plan ahead of time and grasp the visa and entry procedures. Safe travels, and enjoy every moment of your trip to this beautiful part of Turkey!

Traveling to Kuşadası is an adventure, and the route can be as memorable as the destination. Whether you come by air, sea, or car, the prospect of experiencing this stunning coastal town will make the journey much more enjoyable. As you plan your trip, keep these suggestions and options in mind to ensure a smooth and pleasurable journey. Kuşadası offers unforgettable adventures.

Chapter 2

BEST TIME TO VISIT

Weather Overview

When I first arrived in Kuşadası, I was pleasantly surprised by the sunny Mediterranean climate that the town enjoys throughout the year. Kuşadası's weather is one of its most appealing aspects, making it an ideal vacation for any season. Summers here are long, hot, and dry, with temperatures regularly exceeding 30°C (86°F) in July and August. If you enjoy the heat and want to relax on the beach or swim in the Aegean Sea, now is the time for you.

However, spring and autumn have a different, more temperate beauty. During these seasons, the weather is pleasant and warm, with daily temperatures ranging from 20°C to 25°C. The evenings might be cool, so a light jacket may come in helpful. These months are great for visiting the various historical monuments and natural wonders without the summer throng or extreme temperatures. I particularly like May and September since the temperatures were ideal and the flowering flowers or autumn hues brought an extra dimension of beauty to the sceneries.

Winter in Kuşadası is pleasant and refreshing, unlike the harsh winters of northern Europe and North America. The typical temperature is between 10°C and 15°C (50°F to 59°F), and while it can rain, it is never too cold to explore the town and its surrounds. If you prefer a quieter, more serene ambiance, winter may be the best season to visit.

Peak tourist seasons

Kuşadası thrives during peak tourist seasons from June to August. The town is alive with excitement as people from all over the world visit to enjoy the clean beaches, exciting nightlife, and several festivals. During these months, major tourist destinations like as Ephesus and Ladies Beach will see more tourists. Accommodations and flights are typically more expensive, and you'll need to book far in advance to ensure your favorite options.

Despite the crowds, summer in Kuşadası has a unique charm. The long days are wonderful for beach activities, while the warm nights are perfect for exploring the town's vibrant nightlife or attending one of the many cultural events and festivals. The International Kuşadası Festival, held in July, combines music, dancing, and local traditions to showcase the region's vibrant culture.

Offseason Insights

Although the summer months are popular, visiting Kuşadası during the off-season offers unique benefits. From October to April, Kuşadası slows down and offers a more authentic and calm atmosphere. Beaches that are overcrowded during the summer become peaceful sanctuaries. I enjoyed wandering along the beach, listening to the quiet waves, without the congestion and bustle of peak season.

One of the benefits of traveling during the off-season is the chance to explore historical sites without the crowds. Walking through the ancient city of Ephesus during the cooler months was a magical experience. With less tourists present, I was able to really immerse myself in the history and grandeur of this incredible location. Furthermore, local markets and bazaars are less congested, providing for a more leisurely shopping experience and improved contacts with friendly local sellers.

Another advantage of traveling during the off-season is a huge reduction in costs. Flights, lodgings, and even some tourist sites are less expensive, making it an ideal time for budget-conscious tourists. Many hotels and guesthouses featured special deals and discounts, making it possible to stay for less money while still having a good experience.

Choosing the Right Time for You

When to visit Kuşadası is mostly determined by personal tastes and desired outcomes. If you appreciate crowded locations, hot temperatures, and attending festivals and events, the summer months are ideal for you. If you want a slower pace, milder temperatures, and a more cultural experience, consider visiting in the spring, autumn, or even winter.

Spring and autumn are wonderful seasons for outdoor activities such as hiking and exploring nature. The Dilek Peninsula National Park, with its breathtaking paths and diverse animals, is especially beautiful during these months. I recall a spring hike where I was surrounded by flowering wildflowers and had clear views of the Aegean Sea; it was simply breathtaking.

On the other hand, winter may appeal to individuals who value peace and don't mind a little rain. Explore Kuşadası's local cuisine, museums, and pleasant cafes and restaurants. Furthermore, the off-season provides a unique opportunity to see the town from a local's perspective, as daily life moves at a slower pace.

In summary, Kuşadası is a year-round resort that offers something for every season. Whether you like the bustling energy of summer or the tranquil serenity of winter, this lovely town has plenty to offer and explore. To maximize your stay in Kuşadası, plan your visit based on your specific likes and interests.

Chapter 3

DURATION OF STAY

Ideal Length of Stay

When planning a trip to Kuşadası, one of the first things to consider is how long to stay. In my experience, the ideal length of stay in this beautiful coastal town depends largely on what you want to do and see. However, to truly savor the essence of Kuşadası, I recommend at least a week. This allows you to immerse yourself in the culture, explore the main attractions, and have some time to relax on its stunning beaches.

Short Stay (3-4 Days)

For those with limited time, a short stay of 3-4 days can still be incredibly rewarding. This duration is perfect for a quick getaway, offering a taste of Kuşadası's most iconic sights and experiences.

Day 1: Arrival and Initial Exploration

After arriving and settling into your accommodation, take a leisurely stroll through the town. Visit the bustling harbor, where you can watch the boats come and go, and perhaps enjoy a seafood dinner at one of the many waterfront restaurants. The sunset over the Aegean Sea is not to be missed.

Day 2: Historical Sites

Dedicate your second day to exploring the ancient city of Ephesus. This UNESCO World Heritage site is one of Turkey's most significant archaeological wonders. Wander through the ruins of this once-thriving city, marvel at the Library of Celsus, and step into the Grand Theatre, which could hold up to 25,000 spectators.

Day 3: Beach and Relaxation

Spend your third day soaking up the sun at Ladies Beach, one of the most popular spots in Kuşadası. The soft sands and clear waters make it a perfect place to unwind. In the evening, explore Kaleiçi, the old town, with its narrow streets, traditional houses, and quaint shops.

Medium Stay (5-7 Days)

A medium stay of 5-7 days offers a more in-depth experience, allowing you to delve deeper into the attractions and enjoy a mix of relaxation and exploration.

Day 1-3: Initial Exploration and Historical Sites

Follow the itinerary for the short stay to get a comprehensive introduction to Kuşadası and its most famous landmarks.

Day 4: Natural Beauty and Adventure

On the fourth day, venture out to Dilek Peninsula National Park. This stunning natural reserve offers a variety of hiking trails, beautiful beaches, and rich wildlife. It's a fantastic place for nature lovers and those looking to escape the hustle and bustle of town.

Day 5: Pamucak Beach and Sirince Village

Spend your fifth day at Pamucak Beach, a more tranquil alternative to the busier Ladies Beach. After a relaxing morning, head to Sirince Village in the afternoon. This charming village, nestled in the hills, is known for its wine and olive oil. Stroll through the picturesque streets, visit local shops, and enjoy a glass of local wine.

Day 6: Cultural Immersion

Dedicate the sixth day to cultural experiences. Visit the Oleatrium Olive and Olive Oil Museum to learn about the region's rich history with olives. In the evening, attend a local cultural event or festival if one is taking place. These events are a great way to connect with the local culture and traditions.

Day 7: Final Day of Relaxation

Use your last day to revisit any favorite spots or explore new ones you might have missed. Perhaps take a boat tour around the bay, indulge in some last-minute shopping, or simply relax and enjoy the atmosphere.

Extended Stay (8-14 Days)

For those with the luxury of time, an extended stay of 8-14 days allows for a comprehensive exploration of Kuşadası and its surroundings, along with ample relaxation.

Days 1-7: Follow the Medium Stay Itinerary

Start your trip with the medium stay itinerary to cover all the essential experiences and attractions.

Day 8: Boat Excursion

On your eighth day, take a full-day boat excursion. These tours often include stops at various bays and beaches, providing opportunities for swimming, snorkeling, and enjoying the sun. Many tours also include lunch on board, offering a delightful taste of local cuisine.

Day 9: Day Trip to Samos

Consider a day trip to the Greek island of Samos, just a short ferry rides away. Explore the island's beautiful beaches, historical sites, and charming villages. It's a wonderful way to add an international flavor to your Kuşadası adventure.

Day 10: Adventure Activities

For the adventurous, Kuşadası offers activities like paragliding, scuba diving, and horseback riding. Spend your tenth day experiencing the thrill of these activities, taking in the stunning views and underwater wonders of the region.

Day 11: Visit Nearby Cities

Take a day trip to nearby cities such as Selçuk or İzmir. Selçuk is home to more historical sites like the Basilica of St. John and the Temple of Artemis. İzmir, a bustling metropolis, offers a vibrant mix of modern and historical attractions, along with great shopping and dining options.

Day 12: Wellness and Spa Day

Dedicate a day to wellness and relaxation. Many hotels and resorts in Kuşadası offer excellent spa facilities. Treat yourself to a traditional Turkish bath (hamam), massages, and other rejuvenating treatments.

Day 13: Explore Local Villages

Spend a day exploring the lesser-known villages around Kuşadası. Kirazlı Village, for instance, offers a peaceful retreat with its orchards, vineyards, and traditional lifestyle. It's an excellent way to experience the rural charm of Turkey.

Day 14: Leisurely Wrap-Up

Use your final day to revisit your favorite spots, do some last-minute shopping, or simply relax. Enjoy a leisurely breakfast, take a final stroll along the harbor, and soak in the beauty of Kuşadası one last time before departing.

Suggested Stay Durations Based on Interests

History Buffs

If you're a history enthusiast, Kuşadası is a treasure trove of ancient sites and ruins. A stay of at least a week is recommended to fully appreciate the historical wealth of the area. You'll want to spend several days exploring Ephesus, Selçuk, and other nearby archaeological sites.

Itinerary Highlights:

- Ephesus: Spend at least a full day here, possibly more.
- St. John's Basilica and Temple of Artemis in Selçuk.
- House of the Virgin Mary.
- Visits to local museums and historical exhibits.

Beach Lovers

For those who come for the sun and sea, Kuşadası's beautiful beaches are the main draw. A stay of 5-7 days will allow you to enjoy the best of the coastal attractions and have plenty of time for relaxation.

Itinerary Highlights:

- Ladies Beach and Pamucak Beach for sunbathing and swimming.
- Güvercinada Island for scenic views.
- Boat tours to explore hidden coves and beaches.

- Relaxation at beachside cafes and restaurants.

Adventure Seekers

If you're looking for adventure, Kuşadası has plenty to offer. From water sports to hiking and exploring natural parks, an extended stay of 7-10 days will give you ample opportunity to satisfy your adventurous spirit.

Itinerary Highlights:

- Paragliding over the Aegean Sea.
- Scuba diving and snorkeling excursions.
- Hiking in Dilek Peninsula National Park.
- Horseback riding and jeep safaris.

Cultural Enthusiasts

For those who love immersing themselves in local culture, Kuşadası offers a rich blend of traditions, cuisine, and festivals. A stay of at least a week is ideal to experience the cultural depth of the region.

Itinerary Highlights:

- Attending local festivals and events.
- Exploring traditional markets and bazaars.

- Visiting cultural museums and galleries.
- Enjoying traditional Turkish cuisine and cooking classes.

Family Vacationers

Families will find Kuşadası a fantastic destination with activities and attractions suitable for all ages. A stay of 7-10 days ensures a balanced mix of fun and relaxation.

Itinerary Highlights:

- Adaland Aquapark and other family-friendly attractions.
- Beach days at safe and clean beaches.
- Guided tours that are educational and entertaining.
- Leisurely days exploring parks and nature reserves.

Wellness and Relaxation Seekers

If your goal is to unwind and rejuvenate, Kuşadası's serene environment and wellness facilities are perfect. An extended stay of 10-14 days will give you plenty of time to relax and recharge.

Itinerary Highlights:

- Spa days and wellness treatments.
- Yoga and meditation retreats.
- Relaxing beach days and boat tours.
- Visiting serene villages and nature parks for peaceful walks.

In conclusion, the duration of your stay in Kuşadası should align with your interests and what you hope to get out of your trip. Whether you're there for history, adventure, relaxation, or family fun, Kuşadası offers a diverse range of experiences that can be tailored to fit any length of stay. So pack your bags, plan your itinerary, and get ready for an unforgettable journey in this beautiful corner of Turkey!

Chapter 4

TOP TOURIST ATTRACTIONS IN KUŞADASI

Ephesus: Ancient Marvels

When I initially arrived at Ephesus, I felt like I was walking back in time. Ephesus is more than just a tourist destination; it's an intense historical trip. This ancient city, one of the world's best-preserved archeological monuments, provides an intriguing peek into Roman life and architecture. Ephesus, located near the modern town of Selçuk in Turkey's Izmir Province, is easily accessible from Kuşadası and a must-visit for anybody exploring the region.

Getting There

Ephesus is located about 20 kilometers (12 miles) from Kuşadası. The journey by car or taxi takes approximately 25 minutes. If you prefer public transportation, local minibusses (dolmuş) and buses run regularly between Kuşadası and Selçuk, where Ephesus is situated.

Address: Artemis Temple (start point), Atatürk Mahallesi, Dr. Sabri Yayla Bulvarı, No:21, Selçuk, Izmir, Turkey.

Highlights of Ephesus

1. Library of Celsus

Address: Efes Harabeleri, Atatürk Mahallesi, 35920 Selçuk, İzmir, Turkey.

The Library of Celsus is undoubtedly Ephesus' most prominent edifice. This beautiful library, built in the second century AD, was dedicated to Tiberius Julius Celsus Polemaeanus, the governor of Asia. Its two-story front features columns and figures, and it formerly housed thousands of scrolls.

Highlights:

- **Architectural splendor:** The exterior is adorned with intricately carved masonry and statues of the four virtues: wisdom, knowledge, destiny, and valor.
- **Photo Opportunities:** The library's beautiful design makes it an ideal location for photography, particularly during the golden hour.

2. The Great Theatre

Address: Efes Harabeleri, Atatürk Mahallesi, 35920 Selçuk, İzmir, Turkey.

The Great Theatre of Ephesus is a masterpiece of ancient engineering. This gigantic building, which could accommodate up to 25,000 people, was primarily utilized for gladiatorial competitions and theatrical events.

Highlights:

- **Acoustics:** The theatre's design allows even the smallest sound from the stage to be heard throughout the seating area.
- **Panoramic Views:** Climb to the highest tiers for a stunning perspective of the historic city and its surroundings.

3. Temple of Artemis

Address: Artemision, Atatürk Mahallesi, 35920 Selçuk, İzmir, Turkey.

The Temple of Artemis, sometimes called the Artemision, was one of the Seven Wonders of the Ancient World. Although only a single column remains now, the site is rich in history and provides a sense of the temple's vast size.

Highlights:

- Historical Significance: The temple was dedicated to Artemis, the goddess of the hunt, and was once an important religious center.
- Exploration: Wander through the ruins and contemplate the majesty of what once stood here.

4. Terrace Houses

Address: Efes Harabeleri, Atatürk Mahallesi, 35920 Selçuk, İzmir, Turkey.

The Terrace Houses in Ephesus are a collection of opulent houses belonging to the city's wealthy. These homes, often known as the "houses of the rich," are notable for their well-preserved mosaics and frescos.

Highlights:

- **Intricate Mosaics:** The Terrace House floors are adorned with magnificent mosaics depicting images from mythology and daily life.
- **Restoration Work:** The continuous restoration operations shed light on the preservation practices employed to sustain these ancient homes.

5. Curetes Street

Address: Efes Harabeleri, Atatürk Mahallesi, 35920 Selçuk, İzmir, Turkey.

Curetes Street was one of Ephesus' main thoroughfares, replete with statues, monuments, and important structures. Walking down this street provides a vivid picture of life in ancient Ephesus.

Highlights:

- **Historical Buildings:** The Temple of Hadrian and the Gate of Hercules are two notable sites along Curetes Street.
- **Public Spaces:** Explore the remains of ancient public baths and fountains that served Ephesus' people.

6. The Odeon

Address: Efes Harabeleri, Atatürk Mahallesi, 35920 Selçuk, İzmir, Turkey.

The Odeon, a smaller theatre, hosted political gatherings and musical acts. With a seating capacity of approximately 1,500, it is a more intimate venue than the Great Theatre.

Highlights:

- **Well-Preserved Structure:** The Odeon's structure is astonishingly preserved, providing a distinct image of its original appearance.
- **Cultural Importance:** This location was extremely important in Ephesus' civic and cultural life.

Practical Tips for Visiting Ephesus

Opening Hours and Tickets

- Ephesus is open to visitors year-round, with different opening hours depending on the season.
- Summer (April to October): 8:00 AM – 7:00 PM
- Winter (November to March): 8:00 AM – 5:00 PM

Ticket prices:

Adult: Approximately 150 Turkish Lira

- Children under 12: free.
- It's advisable to purchase tickets online in advance, especially during peak tourist seasons, to avoid long queues.

What to Bring

- **Comfortable Footwear:** The location is large, and you will be walking a lot over rough surfaces.

- **Sun Protection:** Hats, sunglasses, and sunscreen are vital, especially during the summer months.
- **Water and Snacks:** There are few facilities on the archeological site, so bring lots of water and small snacks.

Guided tours

- Consider hiring a local guide or going on a guided tour to enhance your experience. Knowledgeable guides may provide detailed historical context and tell captivating anecdotes that bring the ancient city to life.

Nearby Attractions

After exploring Ephesus, there are several additional notable sites in the area that are worth a visit:

1. House of the Virgin Mary

Address: Mount Koressos, Selçuk, İzmir, Turkey.

This sacred spot, considered to be the Virgin Mary's final resting place, is a pilgrimage destination for Christians. Nestled in the tranquil environs of Mount

Koressos, the house provides a peaceful refuge for spiritual thought.

Highlights:

- **Holy Water:** There are taps that supply holy water, which many people gather in little bottles.
- **Wishing Wall:** A wall where pilgrims write their prayers and wishes on pieces of paper.

2. Basilica of St. John

Address: St. Jean Caddesi, 35920 Selçuk, İzmir, Turkey.

The Basilica of St. John is a prominent religious location where John the Apostle is said to be buried. The ruins of the basilica, built by Emperor Justinian in the sixth century, provide insight into early Christian architecture.

Highlights:

- **Scenic Views:** The property provides panoramic views of Selçuk and its surroundings.
- **Historical Insight**: Informative inscriptions and signs explain the basilica's history and significance.

3. Isa Bey Mosque

Address: Şirince Köyü Yolu, 35920 Selçuk, İzmir, Turkey.

Built in 1375, the Isa Bey Mosque is a stunning example of Seljuk architecture. Its exquisite design and serene environment make it an enjoyable halt on your travel.

Highlights:

- **Architectural Beauty:** The mosque's interior features intricate calligraphy and ornate decorations.
- **Cultural Significance:** It is still used for worship, showing the Seljuk era's long-lasting legacy.

Güvercinada: The Pigeon Island

Güvercinada, or Pigeon Island, is one of Kuşadası's crown jewels, offering a unique blend of historical intrigue and natural beauty. This small island is a must-visit for anyone exploring the region. It is connected to the mainland by a lovely causeway, making it easily accessible on foot.

Historical significance

Güvercinada has a rich history dating back to the Byzantine era. The island was strategically important due to its location at the entrance of Kuşadası Bay. The main highlight of the island is the Byzantine fortress, which was later reinforced by the Ottomans to protect the coast from pirate attacks. This historical backdrop adds an element of intrigue to your stay.

The Fortress

Address: Güvercinada Caddesi, Kuşadası, Turkey

Walking up to the fortress is like stepping back in time. As you climb the stone steps, you can almost hear the sounds of previous conflicts. The fortress itself is extremely well-preserved, with high stone walls and tall battlements. The peak offers panoramic views of Kuşadası and the neighboring Aegean Sea. It's an excellent location for photography, especially around sunset when the sky is painted in shades of orange and pink.

Highlights of the Fortress:

- **Panoramic Views:** The views from the fortress are breathtaking. The view includes the entire town of Kuşadası, the busy port, and the stunning Aegean Sea. It's an ideal location for taking great images.

- **Historical Artifacts:** Throughout the fortress, you will find numerous displays and artifacts that depict the narrative of the island's strategic importance over time. Information panels describe the fortress's construction and historical occurrences.
- **Tranquil Atmosphere:** Despite its historical significance, the fortress offers a peaceful atmosphere. It's a nice area to relax and ponder while admiring the island's natural beauty.

Scenic walks

Güvercinada is ideal for leisurely strolls. The island's pathways wind around the stronghold and along the coast, providing breathtaking vistas and opportunities to appreciate the natural environment. The causeway is a beautiful walk, especially when the sea is calm and reflects the blue sky.

Highlights of the Scenic Walks:

- **Coastal Pathways:** These paths are well-kept and allow easy access around the island. Walking along these paths offers views of the rocky coastline, blue waters, and lush flora.

- **Photography Opportunities:** The island is a photographers' paradise. There are plenty of picture-perfect moments to capture, whether it's the rocky beauty of the coast, an intimidating stronghold, or tranquil seascapes.
- **Bird Watching:** Pigeon Island is, as the name implies, a birdwatcher's paradise. Various types of seabirds can be seen here, making it an ideal location for wildlife aficionados.

Marine Life & Snorkeling

The waters of Güvercinada are crystal clear and teeming with marine life, making it an ideal snorkeling destination. On a hot day, nothing beats diving into the refreshing waters and discovering the undersea world.

Highlights of Snorkeling at Güvercinada:

- **Vibrant Marine Life:** The rocky seabed around the island is home to a variety of fish, sea urchins, and other marine creatures. Snorkeling here, I noticed schools of colorful fish racing around the rocks and a few octopuses lurking in cracks.
- **Clear Waters:** The water around Güvercinada is remarkably clear. Visibility is high, allowing for easy observation of the rich marine species.

- **Relaxing Beaches:** After snorkeling, relax on the island's modest, pebbly beaches. It's a fantastic way to spend a warm afternoon, alternating between swimming and relaxing on the beach.

Picnicking and Relaxation

Güvercinada is also an ideal location for a relaxed picnic. The island has various covered locations where you can sit and enjoy your food while taking in the scenery.

Highlights of Picnicking on Güvercinada:

- **Scenic Picnic Spots:** There are several designated picnic areas with benches and tables. These locations give cover and are perfectly positioned to provide breathtaking views of the sea and mainland.
- **Peaceful Environment:** The island is frequently less congested than the mainland, providing a tranqu l respite. Relax and enjoy Kuşadası's natural beauty.
- **Accessibility:** The island is readily reached by foot from the mainland, making it an ideal location for a quick escape from the hustle and bustle of town.

Practical information.

Getting to Güvercinada

- **Location:** The island is connected to the mainland by a causeway that starts near the Kuşadası Marina. It's a short yet lovely walk.
- If you stay in central Kuşadası, the island is easily accessible by foot. For those coming from further afield, local buses and taxis can drop you off near the causeway.
- **Best Time to Visit Spring and Autumn:** These seasons offer mild weather and fewer crowds, making it an ideal time to explore the island.
- **Summer:** While it's the busiest time, summer provides the best conditions for swimming and snorkeling. Simply prepare for hotter heat and more tourists.

Tips for visiting

- **Wear Comfortable Shoes:** The paths around the island can be uneven, so comfortable walking shoes are essential.
- **Bring Water and Snacks:** Because the island has minimal facilities, it's best to bring your own refreshments.
- **Respect the Environment:** As with any natural area, it is critical to respect the environment.

Dispose of rubbish responsibly and avoid disturbing wildlife.

Kaleiçi Mosque: Historical Architecture

The Kaleiçi Mosque, located in Kuşadası's old town, represents the region's rich cultural and religious past. The Ottoman-era mosque in Kuşadası has amazing architectural elements and a tranquil environment, making it a must-see destination. Allow me to take you on a detailed trip of what makes Kaleiçi Mosque unique and why it should be on your schedule.

Architectural Beauty Exterior Design

As you approach Kaleiçi Mosque, located at Mahmut Esat Bozkurt Caddesi No: 8, you'll see its majestic minaret piercing the sky, which is a common aspect of Ottoman architectural design. The mosque's exterior features traditional stonework and ornate sculptures that reflect the creativity of the time. The great wooden doors welcome you into a sanctuary that is both old and sacred.

Interior Elegance

Stepping inside the mosque displays a basic yet magnificent interior. The walls are covered with stunning Iznik tiles, which are noted for their brilliant blue and white designs. These tiles frequently feature floral themes and geometric designs, contributing to the mosque's peaceful atmosphere. The mihrab (prayer niche) is carefully built and directs pilgrims to Mecca. The mosque's interior is filled with soft, natural light that seeps through the stained glass windows, providing a peaceful and contemplative environment.

Cultural Significance

Kaleiçi Mosque is more than just a place of worship; it is also an integral part of the local community. Built in the 17th century, it has seen numerous generations of worshippers and serves as a symbol of perseverance and faith. The mosque's involvement in daily life is evident during prayer times, especially on Fridays, when the call to prayer (adhan) reverberates throughout the old town, attracting people from all walks of life.

Visiting Kaleiçi Mosque

Prayer Times and Visitor Etiquette

The mosque is open to tourists outside of prayer times. To truly appreciate its beauty and significance, it's necessary to remember its main purpose as a place of worship. Visitors should wear modestly, with their shoulders and knees covered. Women are generally expected to cover their heads, and scarves are frequently available at the entrance. Shoes must be removed before entering the prayer hall, therefore choose footwear that is easy to remove.

Guided tours

Those interested in learning more about the mosque's history and architecture can take guided tours. These tours provide useful information on Ottoman architectural style and the historical context in which the mosque was created. I definitely recommend having a tour because it enhances the experience and allows you to appreciate the mosque's unique elements and craftsmanship.

Nearby Attractions

After visiting Kaleiçi Mosque, there are various surrounding things to explore. The old town, or Kaleiçi, is a lovely neighborhood with small lanes, historic buildings, and boutique shops.

Kuşadası Bazaar.

The Kuşadası Bazaar, located a short walk from the mosque, provides a bustling shopping experience. You may find everything here, from handmade crafts and jewelry to spices and fabrics. It's an excellent spot to buy souvenirs and immerse yourself in local culture. The bazaar is located at Atatürk Bulvarı No: 50, Kuşadası.

Old Houses of Kaleiçi

Wandering around the streets of Kaleiçi, you'll see magnificently maintained Ottoman-era residences. These ancient homes, with their wooden balconies and elaborate façade, provide a look into Ottoman architecture and lifestyle. Some of these houses have been turned into cafes or stores, offering a unique backdrop for relaxation and a cup of Turkish tea.

Küçük Ada Kalesi (Pigeon Island Castle).

The causeway to Pigeon Island is within a short walk from the mosque. The island features a Byzantine-era fortification with breathtaking views of the Aegean Sea and Kuşadası. It's an ideal location for a leisurely walk and some fantastic photo opportunities. Pigeon Island's address is Kuşadası, Aydın Province.

Practical Information

- **Address:** Mahmut Esat Bozkurt Caddesi No: 8, Kuşadası, Turkey
- **Opening Hours:** Outside Islamic prayer times, the mosque is normally open from morning until evening. It is preferable to visit after the midday prayer, approximately 1:30 PM.
- **Entry Fee:** There is no entry fee, but donations are appreciated to help with the mosque's upkeep.
- **Best Time to Visit:** Early morning or late afternoon visits are recommended because the mosque is calmer, allowing for a more contemplative experience.

Dilek Peninsula National Park: Nature's Haven

Dilek Peninsula National Park, also known as Büyük Menderes Delta National Park or just Milli Park, is a natural sanctuary that provides the ideal getaway into the wild. This vast park, which spans over 27,000 hectares, is a paradise for nature lovers, hikers, wildlife enthusiasts, and anybody wishing to experience the pristine splendor of Turkey's Aegean area. The park is only 30 kilometers south of Kuşadası, making it a convenient day excursion for guests.

How to Get There

Address: Dilek Peninsula-Büyük Menderes Delta National Park, Güzelçamlı Mahallesi, 09430 Kuşadası/Aydın, Turkey

- **By Car:** From Kuşadası, take the D515 highway south towards Güzelçamlı. The park entrance is clearly marked and easy to discover. There are various parking locations throughout the park.
- **By Public Transport:** Dolmuş (minibuses) run regularly from Kuşadası to Güzelçamlı. The park entrance is only a short walk from the Güzelçamlı dolmuş stop.

Highlights of Dilek Peninsula National Park

1. Hiking Trails

The park has a range of hiking trails suitable for all levels of fitness and expertise. Each trail provides a unique view, ranging from deep pine forests to breathtaking coastline panoramas.

- **Karasu Trail:** This trail leads through lush pine forests and offers panoramic views of the Aegean Sea. The hike is moderate in difficulty and acceptable for the majority of people. Along the trip, you'll see ancient ruins and a wide range of vegetation and fauna.
- **Canyon Trail:** For a more demanding hike, follow the Canyon Trail across the park's harsh terrain. The walk leads through tiny gorges and past cascading cascades. It's a thrilling trip with spectacular sights.
- **Zeus Cave Trail:** This shorter and simpler climb leads to the famous Zeus Cave, a natural grotto with crystal-clear water. According to tradition, Zeus bathed here. It's an ideal location for a refreshing plunge.

2. Wildlife Watching

Dilek Peninsula is home to a diverse range of fauna. While exploring the park, keep an eye out for these amazing creatures:

- **Wild Boars:** These secretive animals are frequently observed foraging in the underbrush. They are often shy and avoid people.
- **Deer:** The park has a healthy population of deer, which can occasionally be seen grazing in the meadows.

- **Birds:** The park is a bird-watcher's dream, with over 250 species documented. Look for the bright blue flash of a kingfisher or the magnificent soar of an eagle.

3. Beaches and bays

The park's shoreline is lined with picturesque beaches and hidden bays ideal for swimming, snorkeling, and sunbathing.

- **Karasu Bay:** One of the park's most picturesque beaches, Karasu Bay is a hidden gem. The water is very clean, making it great for snorkeling. The beach is flanked by pine forests, creating a quiet atmosphere.
- **Aydınlık Beach:** This sandy beach is perfect for families, with gentle waves and plenty of shade. It's an ideal area for a picnic.
- Kavaklıburun Bay is a serene and isolated location ideal for individuals seeking seclusion. The beach is pebbled, and the water is deep and clear, making it ideal for diving.

4. Historical Sites

The park is not simply a natural wonder, but it also has historical value. Ancient remains are scattered throughout the park, telling the narrative of its rich history.

- **Ancient City of Karina:** These ruins are the remains of a once-thriving ancient city. Walking among the decaying walls and columns, I could almost hear the sounds of history. It's a fascinating look at the region's history.
- **Monastery of Agios Antonios:** Perched on a mountainside, this Byzantine monastery provides breathtaking views of the surrounding environment. The ruins are atmospheric, and the hike to them is worthwhile.

Practical information

- **Opening Hours:** The park is open everyday from 8:00 a.m. to 7:00 p.m. It is recommended to visit early in the morning to escape the midday heat and increase your chances of observing wildlife.
- **Entrance Fee:** The park charges a nominal entrance fee, which helps with maintenance and conservation initiatives. As of my previous visit, the charge was approximately 10 Turkish Lira per person, but it is recommended that you verify the current rates before your trip.
- **Facilities:** The park has a variety of amenities for guests. There are various picnic areas with tables and seats, facilities, and dedicated camping sites for people who want to remain overnight.

Tips for visiting

- **Bring Plenty of Water:** Hiking may be difficult, especially in the summer heat. Make sure you have enough water to stay hydrated.
- **Wear Suitable Footwear:** Good hiking boots or sturdy sneakers are recommended, especially for the more challenging trails.
- **Respect wildlife:** Maintain a safe distance from animals and do not feed them. It's critical to respect their natural environment.
- **Leave no trace:** Make sure you take all of your trash with you and leave the park as you found it.

Nearby Attractions

If you have time, there are several other attractions near Dilek Peninsula National Park that are worth visiting:

- **Güzelçamlı Village:** This charming village is the gateway to the park. It's a terrific place to eat traditional Turkish food and buy for local products.
- **Doğanbey Village:** Located just outside the park, Doğanbey is a beautifully preserved Ottoman village. Strolling over its cobblestone streets and

seeing the stone houses seemed like traveling back in time.

Adaland Aquapark: Family Fun

Adaland Aquapark is one of Turkey's largest and most spectacular water parks, providing a day of fun and adventure for families, thrill seekers, and anybody wishing to cool off in the Mediterranean heat. This is a must-see destination for visitors to Kuşadası, conveniently located within a short drive from the city center.

Location and Getting There

Address: Adaland Aquapark, Camlimani Mevkii, 09400 Kuşadası, Aydın, Turkey

Getting to Adaland Aquapark is straightforward. The location is around 7 kilometers north of Kuşadası town center and may be reached by automobile, taxi, or frequent dolmuş (minibus) services. If you're driving, there's plenty of parking accessible on site.

Water Rides and Attractions

Adaland Aquapark offers a wide range of water rides and attractions to suit all ages and degrees of thrill-seeking. Here are a few of the highlights.

Thrill Rides

- **Kamikaze:** This ride is not for the faint-hearted. The Kamikaze is a steep, high-speed slide that provides an exciting plunge into the water below. It's a brief yet exhilarating experience that left me breathless.
- **Black Hole:** As the name implies, this ride is a dark, twisting tube with unexpected twists and turns. It's an exciting ride into the unknown, and the darkness only adds to the adrenaline.
- **Red Phantom:** Another high-speed slide, the Red Phantom takes you down a steep fall with quick twists and turns. The slide's design increases speed and thrill, making it a popular choice among adrenaline enthusiasts.

Family and Kid-Friendly Areas

- **Wave Pool:** The wave pool is ideal for families seeking a simulated ocean experience. The waves fluctuate in size and intensity, making them enjoyable for both young children and adults. I adored floating on a tube while soft waves lapped about me.
- **Lazy River:** For a more peaceful experience, take a leisurely, meandering ride through the park.

Floating around the river in an inflatable tube, I enjoyed the sun and beauty while taking a breather from the more intensive attractions.

- **Children's Pool and Play Area:** Designed for younger visitors, this area includes smaller slides, water fountains, and shallow pools. My kids adored the pirate-themed play area, which had a miniature water castle and splash zones.

Unique attractions

- **Rain Dance:** The Rain Dance is one of Adaland's most unusual attractions. It's a huge area where you may dance to music and lights while being showered with water. It's a fun way to unwind and enjoy a party atmosphere in the park.
- **Adventure River:** This attraction provides a little more adrenaline than the leisurely river. The Adventure River has rapids and quicker currents, delivering an exciting journey via its twists and turns. I felt it to be an excellent combination of thrill and relaxation.

Shows and Entertainment

Adaland Aquapark is more than simply rides; it also features a variety of shows and entertainment alternatives that enhance the overall experience.

- **Dolphin and Sea Lion Show:** One of the highlights of my visit was the dolphin and sea lion show. The presentation takes place in a separate amphitheater and contains spectacular stunts and performances by these sophisticated marine animals. It is both amusing and educational, providing insights into the creatures' behavior and conservation activities.

- **Parrot Show:** Another fun show at the park is the parrot show, where colorful parrots perform tricks and interact with the audience. It's a great experience, particularly for little children who enjoy animals.

Dining and Amenities

Adaland Aquapark provides a variety of eating alternatives to keep you going throughout the day. The park contains various snack bars, cafes, and restaurants that serve a variety of foods and beverages.

- **Snack Bars:** Scattered throughout the park, these serve quick snacks such as hot dogs, hamburgers, fries, and ice cream. They are ideal for taking a quick snack between rides.
- **Cafes and Restaurants:** For a more substantial dinner, the on-site cafes and restaurants provide a variety of alternatives, including Turkish cuisine and international delicacies. I particularly liked the fresh salads and grilled meats at one of the larger eateries.

- **Ice Cream and Dessert Stands:** No trip to a water park is complete without sampling some sweet snacks. The ice cream stands offer a range of flavors, and the dessert stalls serve excellent pastries and sweets.

Practical Information and Tips

- **Opening Hours:** Adaland Aquapark is normally open from late May to early October, with hours ranging from 10:00 AM to 6:00 PM. Check their official website for the most up-to-date information on opening dates and times.
- **Tickets and Pricing:** Tickets are available for purchase at the gate or online. Purchasing tickets online in advance can save you both money and time. Adults, children, and families have varying pricing options, and groups receive discounted rates.
- **What to Bring:** Bring swimsuit, towels, sunscreen, and water shoes if you have them. Lockers are available for hire to keep your items safe while you enjoy the park.
- **Safety and Rules:** Lifeguards are stationed throughout the park to ensure safety, but it's important to follow all posted rules and guidelines. Pay heed to the rides' height and age

requirements to guarantee a safe and fun experience for all.

Nearby Attractions

If you have time, consider exploring some of the neighboring attractions following your visit to Adaland Aquapark:

- **Aqua Fantasy Aquapark:** Located just a short distance from Adaland, Aqua Fantasy provides another fascinating alternative for water enjoyment, complete with its own distinctive rides and attractions.
- **Pamucak Beach:** After a day at the water park, you may want to unwind at Pamucak Beach, which is famed for its long sandy shoreline and calm waves.
- **Kusadasi City Center:** The city center is only a short drive away and includes a variety of shops, restaurants, and historical attractions to visit.

Kusadasi Castle: Historical Fortification

Kusadasi Castle, also known as Barbaros Hayrettin Pasha Castle, is a historical jewel located on Pigeon Island (Güvercinada), which is connected to the mainland of Kuşadası with a lovely causeway. This well-preserved fortress not only allows a deep dive into the region's history, but it also offers breathtaking vistas and a tranquil respite from the hectic town. Let's look at the rich history, architectural marvels, and practical features that make Kusadasi Castle a must-see attraction.

Historical significance

Kusadasi Castle has a long history, reaching back to the Byzantine era. It was originally built as a strategic fortress to safeguard the coastal town from pirate raids and invaders. The castle's defensive value was maintained throughout the Ottoman period, with significant improvements made in the 16th century under the command of the great Ottoman admiral Barbaros Hayrettin Pasha. The stronghold was important in protecting the Aegean shoreline, and its walls have witnessed many historical events and conflicts.

Architectural Features

The castle exemplifies the military design of the time, with high stone walls, powerful towers, and strategically positioned battlements. The main entryway, embellished with antique inscriptions and carvings, foreshadows the grandeur that awaits inside. As you explore the castle, you'll come across several major places and features:

- **Main Gate and Drawbridge:** The castle's entrance is defended with a strong gate and what was once a drawbridge to discourage intruders. The elaborate brickwork and historical engravings here offer a look into the artistry of the time.
- **Inner Courtyard:** Once inside, the large inner courtyard opens up, where soldiers would have assembled and supplies were stored. Today, it serves as a tranquil spot to unwind and enjoy the scenery.
- **Watchtowers and Battlements:** Climbing up the watchtowers offers a unique perspective of the fortification's layout and provides panoramic views of Kuşadası and the Aegean Sea. The battlements, with carefully placed arrow slits, depict the castle guards' defensive methods.
- **Cannon Placements:** Remains of historic cannons that originally defended the fortress may be found around the castle. These historical items are a reminder of the castle's military history and are intriguing to see up close.

Exhibits and displays

Several displays inside the castle highlight the history and culture of Kusadasi and its surroundings:

- **Historical Artifacts:** Display cases contain artifacts discovered in and around the castle, including ancient weapons, pottery, and tools. These objects establish a concrete link to the castle's former inhabitants and defenders.
- **Informative Panels:** Informational panels located around the castle provide insights into the fortress's historical setting, the significance of particular architectural components, and the stories of those who lived and fought here.
- **Cultural Exhibits:** The castle occasionally holds cultural exhibitions and events, including traditional Turkish music performances and local art shows. These events increase the visitor experience while also highlighting the region's cultural history.

Practical Information for Visitors

Address and Access: Kusadasi Castle (Güvercinada) Güvercinada Caddesi, Kuşadası, Aydın, Turkey

The castle is easily accessed from the town center. It's a short walk from the main marina, and the scenic causeway leading to the island adds to the allure of the trip. The trek to the castle is lovely and provides numerous photo possibilities along the way.

Opening Hours and Entry:

- **Opening hours:** The castle is normally open from early morning till sunset. However, hours may change, particularly during off-peak seasons or special events. Check locally or online for the most up-to-date opening times.
- **Entry Fee:** There is typically a small admission fee to access the castle. This fee helps to maintain and preserve the historic place.

Highlights of Visiting Kusadasi Castle

- **Historical Journey:** Walking through the gates of Kusadasi Castle seems like going back in time. The well-preserved walls and towers transport you to a bygone age, providing insight into the region's rich past.
- **Breathtaking Views:** One of the most compelling reasons to visit Kusadasi Castle is the stunning panoramic views it offers. The watchtowers offer panoramic views of Kuşadası,

including the marina and the Aegean Sea. The sunsets seen from here are very stunning.

- **Peaceful Retreat:** Despite being a popular tourist spot, the castle and its surrounding gardens provide a tranquil escape. The rich vegetation and tranquil environment make it an ideal spot for a leisurely stroll or a quiet period of introspection.
- **Photography Opportunities:** The castle's gorgeous position and historical aura make it a photographer's heaven. Whether you're photographing the delicate features of the masonry or the panoramic views of the shoreline, there are several photo opportunities.
- **Family-Friendly Experience:** The castle is an excellent site to visit with your family. Children will love exploring the old defenses and learning about their history, while adults will value the historical significance and natural beauty.

Nearby Attractions

After exploring Kusadasi Castle, there are a few other nearby things worth seeing:

- **Kuşadası Marina:** A short walk from the castle, the marina is a lively area with shops, restaurants, and cafes. It's an excellent place to unwind and eat with a view of the sea.

- **Kaleiçi Old Town:** The historic center of Kuşadası, known as Kaleiçi, is full of charming narrow streets, traditional houses, and local boutiques. It's a lovely place to explore on foot.
- **Ladies Beach:** One of the most popular beaches in Kuşadası, Ladies Beach, is a short drive or a pleasant walk from the castle. It is ideal for a refreshing swim or some seaside leisure.

Kuşadası offers diverse attractions for all travelers. The historic remains of Ephesus, as well as the colorful beaches and natural parks, have something for everyone. Kuşadası is a site I love returning to seek new discoveries and wonderful moments.

Chapter 5

HIDDEN GEMS AND LOCAL FAVORITES

Kuşadası! Nestled on Turkey's Aegean coast, this lovely vacation town has much more to offer than first appears. Beyond the renowned beaches and bustling bazaars, there are hidden gems that provide a deeper connection to the local culture and scenery. Whether you're a first-time visitor or a frequent traveler, these hidden gems will enhance your Kuşadası experience.

Değirmen Yeri Mill: A Cozy Getaway

The Değirmen Yeri Mill is a fascinating historical landmark located in the lush countryside of Kuşadası. This tiny resort provides a unique peek into the region's rich agricultural past while also providing a calm respite from the crowded tourist areas. As you enter this tranquil setting, you'll feel as if you've been transported back in time, surrounded by the calming sounds of nature and the rhythmic hum of the mill.

Location and Address

Address: Değirmen Mevkii, Kirazlı Köyü Yolu Kuşadası, Aydın, Turkey

Getting There

Değirmen Yeri Mill is located approximately 15 kilometers from the center of Kuşadası. The easiest way to get to the mill is by automobile or cab. Take a dolmuş (shared minibus) from Kuşadası to Kirazlı Village, then walk or take a taxi to the mill.

Highlights of Değirmen Yeri Mill

The Historical Mill

Değirmen Yeri Mill features a well-preserved watermill dating back centuries. The mill has been expertly restored to display the original milling process, giving visitors an intriguing glimpse into how grain was ground into flour in the past. The massive wooden gears, stone millstones, and flowing water channels are all still operational, presenting an enthralling presentation of this centuries-old craft.

As you visit the mill, professional advisors are available to explain the history and operation of the machinery. They tell fascinating anecdotes about the mill's involvement in the local community and its place in the region's agricultural history. Watching the mill in action is both educational and intriguing, as the rhythmic movement and sounds create a relaxing atmosphere.

The Surrounding Gardens

The mill is nestled in beautifully planted gardens, providing a peaceful respite from the rush and bustle of everyday life. The gardens are packed with a variety of native plants, flowers, and trees, resulting in a bright and peaceful atmosphere. There are various covered seating places where you can relax and enjoy the serene surroundings, making it an excellent location for a picnic or a quiet day with a good book.

One of the garden's features is a tiny pond filled with ducks and other wildlife. The peaceful sound of the river, mixed with the chirping of birds and the rustling of leaves, contributes to an overall impression of calm. As you walk through the garden, you'll notice informational plaques with intriguing facts about the many plant species and their functions.

The Café

Adjacent to the mill is a cozy café that serves a selection of traditional Turkish teas, coffees, and pastries. The café's menu includes locally sourced foods, such as freshly baked bread prepared with flour milled on-site. The courteous staff is always eager to propose their favorite delights, ensuring that you have a memorable gastronomic experience.

The café's outdoor seating area offers stunning views of the surrounding countryside, making it a perfect place to unwind and enjoy a leisurely meal. Whether you're enjoying a cup of creamy Turkish coffee or a slice of homemade baklava, the café has a relaxed and welcoming ambiance.

Local Crafts and Souvenirs

Değirmen Yeri Mill also contains a small shop where visitors can buy locally manufactured crafts and souvenirs. The shop sells a variety of handmade things, including ceramics, textiles, and jewelry manufactured by local artisans. These one-of-a-kind sculptures are excellent souvenirs of your trip or great gifts for friends and family.

In addition to crafts, the shop sells products prepared with the mill's flour, such as bread mixes, cookies, and baked delicacies. These items are ideal for taking a taste of Kuşadası home.

Educational Workshops

Değirmen Yeri Mill conducts educational workshops on traditional milling and baking skills. These hands-on classes are guided by expert teachers who walk participants through the steps of grinding grain, creating dough, and baking bread. The classes are appropriate for all ages and ability levels, offering a fun and educational experience for families, couples, and single travelers alike.

Participating in a workshop allows you to obtain a better understanding of the mill's history and the craftsmanship required for traditional baking. You'll leave with new skills and a better awareness of the significance of sustaining these traditional practices.

Seasonal Events and Festivals

Değirmen Yeri Mill offers periodic events and festivals to honor the region's cultural and agricultural legacy. These celebrations frequently include live music, folk dance, and traditional cuisine, resulting in a lively and joyous ambiance. Visitors may see local musicians and dancers perform, sample regional cuisine, and take part in participatory activities like olive oil tastings and pottery demonstrations.

Attending one of these events is an excellent way to immerse yourself in the local culture and connect with others. When arranging your visit, make sure to check the mill's event calendar to see if there are any special activities scheduled.

Tips for Visiting Değirmen Yeri Mill

- **Timing Your Visit:** The mill is open year-round, but the ideal times to visit are in the spring and fall, when the weather is pleasant and the gardens are in flower. Weekdays are typically calmer than weekends, making it easier to appreciate the tranquil settings.
- **Wear Comfortable Shoes:** The mill grounds and adjacent gardens are best explored on foot, so make sure you wear comfortable walking shoes.
- **Bring a Camera:** Değirmen Yeri Mill is incredibly picturesque, with plenty of photo opportunities. Don't forget to bring your camera to capture the beauty of the mill, gardens, and surrounding landscape.
- **Plan a Picnic:** The gardens are an ideal place for a picnic, so pack some snacks or a light lunch to enjoy during your stay. If you prefer to buy your food on-site, the café also has takeaway choices.

- **Check for Workshops:** If you want to participate in a workshop, make sure to book ahead of time because these sessions tend to fill up quickly. Check the mill's website or contact them directly for details on forthcoming workshops and how to secure your position.
- **Respect the Environment:** Değirmen Yeri Mill strives to preserve the natural beauty of its surrounds. Please respect the environment by not littering and remaining on designated trails.

Kirazlı Village: Traditional Turkish Charm

Kirazlı Village is a charming location that captures the essence of traditional Turkish rural life. Located just 10 kilometers from Kuşadası, this tiny village offers a calm refuge from the bustling seaside town, providing tourists with an authentic flavor of the region's culture, cuisine, and natural beauty.

Getting to Kirazlı Village

To reach Kirazlı Village from Kuşadası, take a 15-minute journey via the D515 highway. Local dolmuş (minibuses) travel frequently between Kuşadası and Kirazlı, making it easily accessible for anyone without a car.

Address: Kirazlı Köyü, 09400 Kuşadası/Aydın, Turkey

Exploring the Village:

1. Village Market

One of the highlights of Kirazlı is its vibrant village market, held every Saturday. This market is a sensory experience, with a diverse selection of fresh, locally grown produce. From luscious tomatoes and crisp cucumbers to scented herbs and succulent fruits, the market exemplifies the region's lush soil and traditional farming practices. Don't pass up the opportunity to sample some of the local delicacies, such as homemade jams, freshly baked bread, and gözleme, a savory Turkish flatbread filled with cheese, spinach, or ground meat.

Market Address: Kirazlı Köyü, Market Area, 09400 Kuşadası/Aydın, Turkey

2. Traditional Houses

As you walk around the village, you will observe the wonderfully renovated traditional Turkish homes. These lovely cottages, with their whitewashed walls, red-tiled roofs, and wooden shutters, are frequently embellished with colorful flowers and artistic carving. Many of these homes have been turned into guesthouses, providing a comfortable and authentic lodging experience. Staying in one of these guesthouses allows you to fully immerse yourself in the local culture and experience warm Turkish hospitality.

Guesthouse Recommendation:

Kirazlı Konakları Address: Kirazlı Köyü, 09400 Kuşadası/Aydın, Turkey

3. Organic farming

Kirazlı is recognized for its commitment to organic farming, and many local farms welcome visitors. You can learn about ancient agricultural methods, help with the harvest, and even have a farm-to-table meal. Kirazlı Organik Çiftliği is a farm where tourists may explore the orchards, choose fresh fruits, and have a great lunch made with farm-fresh ingredients.

Farm Visit Recommendation:

- **Kirazlı Organik Çiftliği**

Address: Kirazlı Köyü, 09400 Kuşadası/Aydın, Turkey

4. Olive groves and oil production

Kirazlı is surrounded by historic olive groves, and olive oil production plays a vital role in the local economy. Many small, family-owned olive oil companies provide tours and tastings. Zeytinyağı Evi, an olive oil home, offers a unique opportunity to learn about traditional olive oil manufacturing methods and taste many varietals.

Olive Oil House Recommendation:

Zeytinyağı Evi Address: Kirazlı Köyü, 09400 Kuşadası/Aydın, Turkey

5. Local cuisine.

A visit to Kirazlı is incomplete without experiencing the local cuisine. The area has several attractive restaurants and cafes serving traditional Turkish cuisine produced with locally sourced products. Hanımeli Lokantası is a family-run restaurant that serves hearty home-cooked meals and comes highly recommended. You can eat meals like kebabs, mezes, and fresh salads while taking in the warm and pleasant ambiance.

Restaurant recommendation:

- **Hanımeli Lokantası**

Address: Kirazlı Köyü, 09400 Kuşadası/Aydın, Turkey.

6. Cultural Experiences.

For those interested in cultural experiences, Kirazlı offers several opportunities to engage with local traditions. The village offers a variety of festivals and events throughout the year, commemorating everything from harvest season to religious holidays. These gatherings frequently incorporate music, dance, and traditional Turkish cuisine, making them an excellent opportunity to immerse oneself in the region's rich culture.

Festival Highlight: Kirazlı Harvest Festival Time: Typically held in late summer

7. Nature Walks and Hiking

Kirazlı, with its rolling hills and beautiful sceneries, is an ideal location for nature enthusiasts. There are various walking and hiking routes around the area that provide breathtaking views of the countryside and opportunity to see local wildlife. The routes vary in difficulty, making them accessible to hikers of all skill levels. The trail to the nearby village of Çamlık is a popular choice, winding past olive gardens and pine forests.

Hiking Trail Recommendation:

- **Kirazlı to Çamlık Trail**

Starting Point: Kirazlı Village Center

8. Artisan Shops and Local Crafts

Kirazlı has various artisan stores where visitors can buy handmade products and souvenirs. These businesses sell a variety of locally manufactured items, such as ceramics, textiles, and jewelry. Kirazlı Sanat Evi, an art house that showcases local artisans' work, is a great place to find unusual presents.

Artisan Shop Recommendation:

- **Kirazlı Sanat Evi**

Address: Kirazlı Köyü, 09400 Kuşadası/Aydın, Turkey

Practical Tips for Visiting Kirazlı Village

- **Language:** While Turkish is the primary language, many locals in Kirazlı speak basic English, especially those involved in tourism. Learning a few basic Turkish phrases can improve your experience and endear you to the locals.
- **Currency:** The local currency is the Turkish Lira (TRY). It is recommended that you bring extra cash with you because not all restaurants take credit cards.
- **Dress Code:** Kirazlı is a traditional village, so modest attire is preferred when visiting local houses or places of worship.
- **Local Etiquette:** The Turkish people are recognized for their hospitality. When visiting, it is usual to greet people pleasantly, and accepting offers of tea or food is considered kind.
- **Transportation:** While walking is the easiest method to see the hamlet, having a car is useful for exploring other locations. There is abundant parking in the village.

Oleatrium: Olive and Olive Oil Museum

If you want to learn more about olive oil, you should visit Oleatrium, the Olive and Olive Oil Museum. The Oleatrium, located in Davutlar, a short drive from Kuşadası, provides a unique opportunity to learn about one of the Mediterranean's most popular agricultural products.

Location and Getting There

The Oleatrium is located in Atatürk Mahallesi, Yörük Cad. No:1, Davutlar, Kuşadası. The 15-minute journey from the center of Kuşadası makes it a convenient day getaway. If you do not have your own vehicle, local buses and taxis are easily accessible.

Museum highlights

1. Historical Artifacts and Exhibits.

As you enter the Oleatrium, you are met by a wonderfully renovated edifice that emanates elegance and history. The museum's interior is a beautiful blend of classic and modern design, producing a welcoming environment that transports you to the world of olive oil.

The first portion of the museum is dedicated to historical items from olive agriculture and oil processing. You'll find ancient olive presses, agricultural equipment, and numerous containers used over the centuries to keep this precious oil. Each artifact is accompanied by thorough descriptions that provide context for its historical and cultural value.

2. Olive Oil Production Process

One of the most fascinating aspects of the museum is the portion that takes you through the olive oil producing process. The exhibitions are both instructive and fascinating, covering everything from olive harvesting to pressing and bottling the oil. Interactive displays allow you to observe and experience the various stages of production. There is even a reproduction of a traditional olive press where you can see how olive oil was created in ancient times.

3. Olive Oil Tasting Room

No visit to the Oleatrium is complete without a stop at the tasting room. Here, you can try a selection of olive oils, each with its own distinct flavor character.

The tasting experience is led by knowledgeable professionals who explain the differences between various types of olive oil, how to taste them correctly, and what to look for in high-quality oil. You'll learn to appreciate the unique flavors and aromas that distinguish each olive oil.

4. The Olive Garden

Step outside into the museum's stunning olive garden, where rows of ancient olive trees serve as living reminders of the region's agricultural legacy. The garden is a tranquil and lovely place ideal for a leisurely stroll. There are also informative signage explaining the various types of olive trees and their properties.

5. Workshops & Events

The Oleatrium often conducts workshops and events that delve further into the topic of olive oil. From cooking courses where you can learn how to make traditional Turkish foods with olive oil to seminars on the health benefits of olive oil, these events provide hands-on learning experiences that are both enjoyable and enlightening. Check the museum's schedule to see what activities are coming up.

6. Museum Shop

Before leaving, make sure to stop by the museum shop. You may buy a variety of products created with the museum's olive oil here, including bottles of extra virgin olive oil, handmade soaps, and other olive-based products. These are great keepsakes or gifts for friends and family back home.

7. Guided Tours

For a more in-depth experience, arrange a guided tour of the museum. The educated interpreters will provide extra context and tales about the displays, helping you better understand and appreciate the olive oil production process. Tours can be personalized to your specific interests, whether you're a history buff, a foodie, or just inquisitive about olive oil.

Practical information

- **Opening Hours:** The Oleatrium is open daily from 9:00 a.m. to 5:00 p.m. However, it's always a good idea to check their website or phone beforehand to confirm the hours, which may change during holidays or special events.
- **Admission Fees:** The admission fee is quite reasonable and varies for adults, children, and groups. Discounts are frequently provided for

students and elders. The museum occasionally provides free admission days or special discounts, so check their website or social media pages for current deals.

- **Accessibility:** The museum is wheelchair accessible, including ramps and elevators to ensure that all visitors can comfortably view the exhibits. If you have any special accessibility requirements, please contact the museum in advance to ensure that they can accommodate you.

Tips for Visitors:

- **Plan Your Visit:** Allow at least two hours to visit the museum properly. If you intend to join a workshop or guided tour, you may wish to allow more time.
- **Stay Hydrated:** Staying hydrated is especially important during the warmer months. The museum offers a café where visitors can buy drinks and light food.
- **Engage with the Staff:** The museum staff is extremely knowledgable and passionate about olive oil. Don't be afraid to ask questions or seek recommendations; they'll be pleased to offer their knowledge.

- **Combine with Nearby Attractions:** The Oleatrium is close to several other Davutlar attractions, such as local markets and gorgeous beaches. To make the most of your stay, combine it with a trip to one of these nearby attractions.
- **Respect the Environment:** As with any visit to natural or historical monuments, be aware of your surroundings. Avoid handling the exhibits and make sure all rubbish is properly disposed of.

Pamucak Beach: Unwind in Serenity

Pamucak Beach, located about 10 kilometers north of Kuşadası, offers a peaceful respite from the busy tourist attractions. This large, golden sandy beach spans for over 5 kilometers, providing ample room for leisure and pleasure. Pamucak Beach is well-known for its pristine natural beauty, making it ideal for individuals seeking peace and connection with nature.

Getting There

Pamucak Beach is easily accessible by car or public transport. To reach Pamucak by car, take the D515 highway north from Kuşadası. The journey takes approximately 15-20 minutes. Local dolmuş (minibuses) offer a cost-effective and convenient way to get from Kuşadası to Pamucak.

Address: Pamucak Sahili, 35920 Selçuk/İzmir, Turkey

Highlights of Pamucak Beach

Unspoiled Natural Beauty

One of Pamucak Beach's most enticing features is its pure surroundings. The beach is bordered by sand dunes and rich greenery, creating a gorgeous scene ideal for relaxation. Unlike the other developed beaches in the area, Pamucak has retained its natural appeal, making it a paradise for nature enthusiasts.

Family-friendly atmosphere

Pamucak Beach is a great option for families. The wide, gently sloping shoreline and shallow waves provide a safe and pleasurable environment for youngsters to play and swim. The beach's broad breadth allows families to spread out and enjoy their day without feeling crowded.

Water Sports and Activities

Pamucak Beach provides a variety of water sports for those who are more adventurous. The steady winds and waves make it a popular location for windsurfing and kiteboarding. Several local businesses provide equipment rentals and courses for beginners. Additionally, the tranquil seas near the coast are ideal for paddleboarding and kayaking.

Horseback Riding

Horseback riding down the shore is one of Pamucak Beach's most distinctive experiences. Several local stables provide guided rides, letting you to see the beautiful seaside scenery from a different angle. This exercise is appropriate for all skill levels, including beginners and experienced riders.

Address: Pamucak Horse Club, Pamucak Sahili, 35920 Selçuk/İzmir, Turkey

Picnicking and Relaxation

Pamucak Beach is the best location for a relaxed picnic. The natural dunes provide covered locations where you may have a picnic and enjoy the peaceful surroundings. Bring along some local goodies from the adjacent Selçuk market, such as fresh bread, cheese, olives, and fruits, for a delicious supper by the sea.

Dilek Peninsula National Park

The Dilek Peninsula National Park, located near Pamucak Beach, is a protected region recognized for its rich flora and animals. After a day of sunbathing and swimming, head into the park to discover its scenic hiking routes, picturesque vistas, and secret coves. The park is home to several species of wildlife, including wild boars, deer, and a variety of bird species, making it an ideal location for nature lovers.

Address: Dilek Peninsula National Park, Güzelçamlı Mahallesi, 09430 Kuşadası/Aydın, Turkey

Local Amenities

While Pamucak Beach is less developed than other beaches in the vicinity, it still provides needed amenities for a relaxing day out. There are a few small cafés and snack bars to purchase refreshments, as well as restrooms and showers for your convenience. During high season, you can also hire sunbeds and umbrellas.

Tips for visiting Pamucak Beach

- **Bring Essentials:** While the beach has some conveniences, it's a good idea to bring your own supplies like water, food, and sunscreen, especially if you plan on spending the entire day there.

- **Arrive Early:** To get a decent place, especially during peak season, arrive early in the morning. This will also allow you to visit the beach during cooler, less congested times.
- **Respect Nature:** Pamucak Beach is noted for its natural beauty, so please respect the environment by not leaving any rubbish behind and avoiding upsetting the local fauna.
- **Check the Weather:** Wind conditions might change, so some days are better for water activities than others. If you plan on windsurfing or kiteboarding, check the weather forecast and wind conditions first.
- **Stay Safe:** While the waters are generally safe for swimming, always be mindful of currents and keep an eye on children at all times. During high season, there are generally lifeguards on duty, but it is always a good idea to exercise caution.

In conclusion, Kuşadası is a treasure trove of hidden jewels and local favorites, offering a deeper and more authentic experience of this lovely region. Explore off-the-beaten-path destinations such as Değirmen Yeri Mill, Kirazlı Village, Oleatrium, and Pamucak Beach for unforgettable experiences.

Discover the authentic heart of Kuşadası by venturing beyond the typical tourist locations. You'll be glad you did.

Chapter 6

CULTURAL EXPERIENCES IN KUŞADASI, TURKEY

Turkish Cuisine: A Culinary Adventure

I was initially drawn to Kuşadası's bustling food scene. Turkish food is a sensory trip that features a diverse range of flavors, aromas, and textures. The foods here have a lovely blend of Mediterranean, Middle Eastern, and Central Asian elements. Here are some must-try culinary treats you can't miss in Kuşadası.

Breakfast: Kahvaltı – A Feast to Start Your Day

Kahvaltı, a typical Turkish breakfast, is a must-try experience. It is more than just a meal; it is a ritual. Imagine yourself seated at a table laden with little plates of cheeses, olives, tomatoes, cucumbers, eggs, various spreads, honey, and, of course, freshly made bread. Each bite is a perfect blend of tastes. My particular favorite is simit, a sesame-encrusted bread ring that is commonly served with a strong cup of Turkish tea. Don't miss out on menemen, a delicious scrambled egg dish with tomatoes, green peppers, and spices.

Street Food: Quick Bite Full of flavor.

While exploring Kuşadası's lively streets, you will come across a variety of street food vendors. One piece of gözleme, a delectable Turkish flatbread filled with cheese, spinach, or minced meat, will have you hooked. Another popular dish is döner kebab, which is succulent beef slow-cooked on a vertical rotisserie and often served on pita bread with fresh vegetables and sauces. For a sweet treat, consider baklava, which consists of layers of flaky pastry filled with nuts and sweetened with honey or syrup.

Meze - A Symphony of Small Plates

When dining out, especially at supper, you'll often begin with meze, which is a collection of tiny dishes given as appetizers. It's a terrific opportunity to try new cuisines and share with friends. Some of the highlights include hummus, stuffed grape leaves (dolma), and muhammara, a spicy red pepper and walnut dip. I enjoy cacık, a yogurt and cucumber dip with garlic and mint, for its pleasant flavor. These dishes perfectly set the tone for the main course.

Main Courses: Hearty and Satisfying

Kuşadası provides many main course selections. One standout meal is testi kebab, a savory meat stew prepared in a sealed clay pot and cracked apart at the table. It's a stunning sight and a fantastic supper. If you adore seafood, don't miss out on grilled fish, especially seabass or sea bream, which are freshly caught and lightly seasoned to let the natural flavors show. For a heartier meal, try İskender kebab, thinly sliced lamb served over pita bread, topped with tomato sauce, and drizzled with melted butter and yogurt. It's comfort food at its finest.

Dessert: Sweet Endings

Turkish pastries are ideal for people with a sweet craving. Aside from baklava, which I have already mentioned, you should try künefe, a dessert comprised of shredded pastry drenched in syrup, covered with cheese, and baked till golden and crispy. It is served hot, usually with a dollop of clotted cream on top. Another favorite of mine is lokma, which are small fried dough balls soaked in syrup. They're crispy on the outside and soft on the inside, and they're absolutely delicious.

Traditional Markets and Bazaars

Exploring Kuşadası's culture requires visiting local marketplaces and bazaars. These bustling marketplaces are sensory overload, with the sounds of bargaining merchants, the rich colors of spices and textiles, and the alluring aromas of street cuisine. Allow me to tour you through some of the nicest markets in town.

Kuşadası Bazaar is a shoppers' paradise.

Kuşadası Bazaar, also known as the Grand Bazaar, is a labyrinth of narrow lanes lined with stores offering souvenirs, jewelry, apparel, and leather items. It's an excellent place to find unique gifts and hone your negotiating abilities. Traditional Turkish carpets and rugs are always a favorite of mine because of their amazing craftsmanship. You'll also find a diverse selection of spices, teas, and chocolates that make ideal keepsakes.

Tuesday Market: Fresh Produce and Local Goods

For a more authentic experience, visit the Tuesday Market. Kuşadası's lively market is a popular spot for weekly shopping and a glimpse into local life. Fresh fruits and vegetables, cheeses, olives, and a variety of spices are all available here. The smell of fresh herbs is enticing. I enjoy buying local cheeses and olives here since the quality is excellent. It's also a terrific place to pick up handmade items like textiles and pottery.

Leather and Jewelry Shopping: Craftsmanship at Its Best.

Kuşadası is known for its leather products and jewelry. Many of the bazaar's businesses sell high-quality leather jackets, bags, and shoes. The craftsmanship is excellent, and there are frequently one-of-a-kind patterns that you will not find anywhere else. The jewelry shops are equally stunning, with a diverse selection of gold and silver items, many embellished with valuable stones. It's worth taking your time to browse and find that perfect piece.

Local Festivals and Events

Experiencing local festivals and events is a fantastic way to immerse yourself in the culture of Kuşadası. These celebrations offer a glimpse into the traditions and community spirit of the town. Here are a few that stand out.

Ephesus Festival: A Celebration of History and Culture

The Ephesus Festival is one of the most anticipated cultural events in the region. This festival celebrates the rich history and cultural heritage of the ancient city of Ephesus, which is just a short drive from Kuşadası. The festival usually takes place in late spring or early summer, attracting both locals and tourists alike.

Highlights of the Ephesus Festival:

- **Classical Music Concerts:** One of the most magical experiences is attending a classical music concert in the Great Theatre of Ephesus. This ancient amphitheater, with its remarkable acoustics, provides a stunning backdrop for performances by world-renowned orchestras and soloists. The combination of beautiful music and historic surroundings creates an unforgettable experience.
- **Theatrical Performances:** The festival also features theatrical productions, often inspired by ancient Greek and Roman plays. These performances bring the history of Ephesus to life, allowing you to imagine what it might have been like to live in this ancient city.
- **Art Exhibitions:** Throughout the festival, various art exhibitions are held in and around Ephesus. These exhibitions showcase the works of local and international artists, often focusing on

themes related to the history and culture of the region.

- **Workshops and Lectures:** For those interested in learning more about the history and archaeology of Ephesus, the festival offers workshops and lectures by experts in the field. These sessions provide in-depth insights into the significance of Ephesus and its role in ancient history.

Selçuk Camel Wrestling Festival: A Unique Tradition

One of the most unique and fascinating events you can experience near Kuşadası is the Selçuk Camel Wrestling Festival. Held annually in the nearby town of Selçuk, this traditional event dates back centuries and is deeply rooted in Turkish culture.

What to Expect at the Camel Wrestling Festival:

- **Camel Wrestling Matches:** The main attraction of the festival is, of course, the camel wrestling matches. These matches involve specially trained camels, known as Tülü camels, who are bred for wrestling. The camels are pitted against each other in a controlled environment, with the aim of one camel making the other kneel or flee.

The matches are conducted with strict rules to ensure the safety of the animals.

- **Festive Atmosphere:** The festival is a lively affair, with a carnival-like atmosphere. There are food stalls selling traditional Turkish snacks and drinks, as well as vendors offering souvenirs and crafts. You can enjoy live music, folk dances, and other performances throughout the day.
- **Community Gathering:** The festival is a significant social event for the local community. Families and friends gather to watch the matches, socialize, and celebrate their heritage. As a visitor, you'll have the opportunity to mingle with locals and learn more about this unique tradition.

Local Music and Dance Performances: Feel the Rhythm

Kuşadası is a town that loves to celebrate its culture through music and dance. Throughout the year, you can find various performances that showcase traditional Turkish music and dance, providing a deeper understanding of the region's cultural heritage.

Music Performances:

- **Turkish Folk Music:** One of the most enchanting aspects of Turkish culture is its folk music.

Traditional Turkish folk music often features instruments such as the saz (a type of stringed instrument), the darbuka (a type of drum), and the ney (a type of flute). The melodies are both haunting and beautiful, reflecting the soul of the Turkish people. Look out for performances in local squares or cultural centers.

- **Classical Turkish Music:** For a more refined musical experience, attend a performance of classical Turkish music. This genre, which includes Ottoman court music, features sophisticated compositions and a variety of traditional instruments. Concerts are often held in cultural venues or historic sites, adding to the ambiance.

Dance Performances:

- **Folk Dances:** Traditional Turkish folk dances are vibrant and energetic, often performed in colorful costumes. One of the most popular dances is the Zeybek, native to the Aegean region. It's a solo male dance characterized by slow, measured movements, followed by bursts of energy. Other folk dances include the Halay and the Horon, each with its own unique style and rhythm.
- **Belly Dancing:** Belly dancing, or "Oryantal dans," is another iconic element of Turkish culture. You can often find belly dance performances in local

restaurants or at special events. The dancers' graceful movements and elaborate costumes make for a mesmerizing show.

Religious Festivals: A Blend of Tradition and Spirituality

In addition to cultural festivals, Kuşadası also celebrates various religious festivals that offer a glimpse into the spiritual side of Turkish life.

Ramadan and Eid:

- **Ramadan:** Ramadan is the holy month of fasting in Islam, observed by Muslims worldwide, including in Kuşadası. During this month, Muslims fast from dawn to sunset. It's a time of spiritual reflection, prayer, and community. As a visitor, you'll notice a quieter atmosphere during the day, but after sunset, the town comes alive with Iftar (the breaking of the fast) celebrations. Many restaurants offer special Iftar menus, and it's a great opportunity to join locals in this communal meal.
- **Eid al-Fitr:** At the end of Ramadan, Muslims celebrate Eid al-Fitr, a joyous festival that marks the end of fasting. The celebration includes special prayers, feasting, and giving of gifts. It's a

time of joy and generosity, and you'll find a festive atmosphere throughout Kuşadası. Visiting during Eid provides a unique opportunity to experience the warmth and hospitality of the local community.

Kurban Bayramı (Eid al-Adha):

- **Eid al-Adha:** Also known as the Feast of Sacrifice, Eid al-Adha is another significant Islamic festival. It commemorates the willingness of Ibrahim (Abraham) to sacrifice his son in obedience to God. Families traditionally sacrifice an animal, such as a sheep or goat, and the meat is shared with family, friends, and those in need. The festival includes communal prayers, feasting, and acts of charity. As a visitor, you may have the chance to observe or even participate in some of the festivities.

National Holidays: Celebrating Turkish Pride

Turkey has several national holidays that are celebrated with great enthusiasm across the country, including in Kuşadası.

Republic Day:

- **October 29th:** Republic Day marks the anniversary of the founding of the Turkish Republic in 1923. The day is celebrated with various events, including parades, concerts, and fireworks. In Kuşadası, you'll find a festive atmosphere, with decorations, flag displays, and public celebrations. It's a wonderful time to witness the national pride and joy of the Turkish people.

Victory Day:

- **August 30th:** Victory Day commemorates the victory in the Battle of Dumlupınar, which was a crucial battle during the Turkish War of Independence. The day is marked with military parades, ceremonies, and various cultural events. In Kuşadası, you can attend public events and join in the celebrations.

Harvest Festivals: Celebrating Nature's Bounty

The fertile lands around Kuşadası are known for producing a variety of fruits and vegetables, and the harvest is often celebrated with festivals.

Olive Harvest Festival:

- **October:** The Olive Harvest Festival is a celebration of the olive harvest, an important event for the region's olive oil producers. The festival includes olive-picking activities, cooking demonstrations, and tastings of olive oil and other olive products. You'll also find traditional music and dance performances, as well as stalls selling local crafts and produce. It's a great way to learn about the significance of olives in Turkish culture and enjoy some delicious food.

Grape Harvest Festival:

- **September:** Another notable festival is the Grape Harvest Festival, which celebrates the grape harvest season. The festival features grape-picking activities, wine tastings, and various cultural events. You can enjoy local wines and learn about the winemaking process. The festival also includes music, dance, and plenty of delicious food.

Annual Events and Celebrations

Kuşadası hosts a variety of annual events that cater to different interests, from sports and arts to food and nature.

Kuşadası International Golf Festival:

- **May:** Golf enthusiasts will enjoy the Kuşadası International Golf Festival, held at the Kusadasi International Golf Club. The festival attracts golfers from around the world and includes various competitions, social events, and opportunities to enjoy the stunning golf course with its beautiful views of the Aegean Sea.

Kuşadası Book Fair:

- **July:** For book lovers, the Kuşadası Book Fair is a must-visit event. The fair features book stalls, author signings, and various literary events. It's a great opportunity to discover Turkish literature and meet both local and international authors.

Kuşadası Gastronomy Festival:

- **September:** Foodies will delight in the Kuşadası Gastronomy Festival, which celebrates the rich culinary heritage of the region. The festival includes cooking demonstrations, food tastings, and competitions. You can sample a wide variety of local dishes and learn about the culinary traditions of Kuşadası.

Tips for Attending Festivals and Events

- **Plan Ahead:** Check the dates and schedule of festivals and events before your trip. Some festivals, like the Selçuk Camel Wrestling Festival, have fixed dates, while others may vary each year.
- **Arrive Early:** Festivals can get crowded, so it's a good idea to arrive early to find a good spot and fully enjoy the activities.
- **Dress Comfortably:** Wear comfortable clothing and shoes, especially if you'll be spending a lot of time walking or standing.
- **Stay Hydrated:** Carry water with you, especially if you're attending outdoor events during the warmer months.
- **Be Respectful**: Remember to respect local customs and traditions, and be mindful of the rules and guidelines of each festival or event.

Cultural Etiquette and Basic Phrases

Understanding and respecting local customs is crucial when visiting a new place. In Kuşadası, as in the rest of Turkey, there are certain cultural norms and etiquette that will help you navigate social interactions smoothly.

Greeting and Hospitality: Warm and Welcoming

Turks are known for their hospitality, and you'll often be greeted with warmth and friendliness. A common greeting is a handshake, sometimes accompanied by a slight bow of the head. When meeting someone for the first time, it's polite to say "Merhaba" (Hello). If you're invited to someone's home, it's customary to bring a small gift, such as sweets or flowers, as a token of appreciation.

Dress Code: Modesty and Respect

While Kuşadası is a tourist-friendly town, it's still important to dress modestly, especially when visiting religious sites. For men, this means avoiding sleeveless shirts and shorts, while women should cover their shoulders and knees. Carrying a scarf to cover your head when entering mosques is also a good practice.

Dining Etiquette: Enjoying the Meal

Turkish dining is a social affair, and meals are often enjoyed with family and friends. When invited to a meal, it's polite to wait for the host to indicate where you should sit. It's also customary to wait for the eldest person to start eating before you begin. During the meal, take your time and savor the food

– Turkish cuisine is meant to be enjoyed slowly. If you're served tea or coffee, it's polite to accept it, as it's a sign of hospitality.

Basic Phrases: Connecting with Locals

Learning a few basic Turkish phrases can go a long way in making your interactions with locals more enjoyable. Here are some useful ones:

- Hello: Merhaba
- Thank you: Teşekkür ederim
- Please: Lütfen
- Yes: Evet
- No: Hayır
- Excuse me/Sorry: Afedersiniz
- How much is this?: Bu ne kadar?

Using these phrases, even if your pronunciation isn't perfect, will be appreciated by the locals and can lead to more meaningful connections.

In conclusion, immersing yourself in the cultural experiences of Kuşadası will make your visit truly memorable. From savoring the local cuisine to exploring bustling markets, participating in vibrant festivals, and understanding cultural etiquette, each aspect adds a unique layer to your travel adventure.

So go ahead, dive into the culture, and enjoy every moment in this beautiful Turkish town.

Chapter 7

ITINERARIES FOR EVERY TRAVELER

Kuşadası, Turkey, is a captivating destination brimming with history, culture, and natural beauty. Whether you're visiting for the first time or returning for another adventure, this charming coastal town offers something for everyone. I've crafted several itineraries to help you make the most of your stay, tailored to different interests and travel styles.

Three-Day Itinerary: Highlights of Kuşadası

Day 1: Exploring the Ancient Marvels

Morning: Ephesus

Start your journey with a visit to the ancient city of Ephesus, one of the most well-preserved classical cities in the world. Wander through the Marble Street, admire the grandeur of the Library of Celsus, and stand in awe at the Great Theatre, which once seated 25,000 spectators. Don't forget to visit the Temple of Artemis, one of the Seven Wonders of the Ancient World.

Afternoon: Terrace Houses

After a morning of exploration, head to the Terrace Houses within Ephesus. These well-preserved homes offer a glimpse into the opulent lifestyles of the ancient elite, with their intricate mosaics and frescoes.

Evening: Ladies Beach

End your first day at Ladies Beach, a popular spot for both locals and tourists. Enjoy a leisurely stroll along the promenade, dip your toes in the warm Aegean waters, and savor a delicious seafood dinner at one of the beachside restaurants as you watch the sunset.

Day 2: Nature and Relaxation

Morning: Dilek Peninsula National Park

Spend the morning exploring the stunning Dilek Peninsula National Park. Hike through the lush trails, take in the breathtaking views of the Aegean Sea, and perhaps spot some of the local wildlife. Don't miss the chance to swim in the crystal-clear waters of the secluded bays.

Afternoon: Güvercinada (Pigeon Island)

Return to Kuşadası and visit Güvercinada, a small island connected to the mainland by a causeway. Explore the medieval fortress, enjoy the panoramic views, and relax in the tranquil surroundings.

Evening: Kusadasi Castle

Head back to the mainland and visit Kusadasi Castle. This historical fortification offers incredible views of the harbor and town. It's a great place to take some memorable photos as the sun sets.

Day 3: Cultural Immersion and Shopping

Morning: Kaleiçi Mosque and Old Town

Start your day with a visit to Kaleiçi Mosque, an Ottoman-era mosque with beautiful architecture. Then, wander through the narrow streets of the old town, where you can find charming shops selling local crafts and souvenirs.

Afternoon: Local Markets and Bazaars

Immerse yourself in the local culture by visiting one of Kuşadası's bustling markets. The weekly market near the city center is perfect for picking up fresh produce, spices, textiles, and handmade goods. Don't forget to haggle for the best prices!

Evening: Turkish Dinner and Traditional Entertainment

Wrap up your trip with a traditional Turkish dinner. Choose a restaurant that offers live music or a belly dancing show to complete your cultural experience. Indulge in mezes, kebabs, and baklava as you enjoy the vibrant atmosphere.

Seven-Day Itinerary: In-Depth Exploration

Day 1: Arrival and Orientation

Morning: Arrival and Hotel Check-In

Arrive in Kuşadası and check into your hotel. Take some time to settle in and freshen up after your journey.

Afternoon: Orientation Tour

Get acquainted with Kuşadası with a guided orientation tour. Learn about the town's history, key landmarks, and cultural highlights.

Evening: Welcome Dinner

Enjoy a welcome dinner at a local restaurant, savoring traditional Turkish cuisine and getting to know your fellow travelers.

Day 2: Ancient Wonders

Full Day: Ephesus and Terrace Houses

Dedicate an entire day to thoroughly explore Ephesus and the Terrace Houses. Take your time to absorb the history and architecture of this magnificent site.

Evening: Reflective Walk

After a day of ancient wonders, take a leisurely walk along the harbor, reflecting on the day's discoveries.

Day 3: Nature and Adventure

Morning: Jeep Safari in Dilek Peninsula National Park

Experience the rugged beauty of Dilek Peninsula National Park with a jeep safari. Enjoy the off-road adventure and the stunning natural landscapes.

Afternoon: Pamucak Beach

Relax at Pamucak Beach, known for its serene ambiance and pristine sands. It's a perfect spot for sunbathing and swimming.

Evening: Dinner at the Marina

Dine at one of the restaurants in the marina, where you can enjoy fresh seafood and a beautiful view of the yachts.

Day 4: Cultural Exploration

Morning: Sirince Village

Take a short trip to the charming village of Sirince. Wander through its narrow streets, visit local wineries, and enjoy the peaceful countryside.

Afternoon: Ephesus Museum

Return to Kuşadası and visit the Ephesus Museum to see artifacts from the ancient city, including statues, mosaics, and everyday items.

Evening: Turkish Bath Experience

Unwind with a traditional Turkish bath (hamam) experience. Enjoy the cleansing and relaxation rituals that have been part of Turkish culture for centuries.

Day 5: Beach and Leisure

Morning: Long Beach

Spend the morning at Long Beach, a beautiful stretch of sand perfect for swimming and sunbathing.

Afternoon: Adaland Aquapark

For some family-friendly fun, head to Adaland Aquapark. With its exciting water slides, lazy river, and wave pool, it's a great place to cool off and enjoy some thrills.

Evening: Sunset Cruise

End your day with a sunset cruise along the coast. Enjoy the stunning views, live music, and a delicious dinner on board.

Day 6: Shopping and Local Flavors

Morning: Local Markets

Spend the morning exploring the local markets and bazaars. Pick up some souvenirs, spices, and textiles to take home.

Afternoon: Cooking Class

Join a cooking class to learn how to prepare traditional Turkish dishes. Enjoy the fruits of your labor with a delightful lunch.

Evening: Nightlife Exploration

Discover the vibrant nightlife of Kuşadası. Visit a few bars and nightclubs, or enjoy a relaxed evening at a waterfront café.

Day 7: Relaxation and Departure

Morning: Leisure Time

Spend your final morning at leisure. Enjoy a late breakfast, take a walk along the beach, or visit any last-minute sights.

Afternoon: Packing and Check-Out

Pack your bags, check out of your hotel, and prepare for your departure.

Evening: Farewell Dinner

Before you leave, enjoy a farewell dinner at a local restaurant. Reflect on your wonderful experiences in Kuşadası and start planning your next visit.

Family-Friendly Itinerary

Day 1: Arrival and Family Orientation

Morning: Arrival and Hotel Check-In

Arrive in Kuşadası and check into a family-friendly hotel. Choose accommodations with amenities like a pool and kid-friendly activities.

Afternoon: Orientation Tour

Get to know the area with a family-oriented orientation tour. Highlight spots that kids will love, such as parks and playgrounds.

Evening: Family Dinner

Enjoy a family dinner at a restaurant with a children's menu and entertainment options.

Day 2: Fun and Adventure

Morning: Adaland Aquapark

Spend the day at Adaland Aquapark. The kids will love the water slides, wave pool, and lazy river.

Afternoon: Dolphin and Sea Park

After the aquapark, head to the adjoining Dolphin and Sea Park for a chance to see dolphins, sea lions, and other marine life.

Evening: Beach Time

Relax at the beach in the evening. Build sandcastles, play beach games, and enjoy the sunset together.

Day 3: Educational and Entertaining

Morning: Ephesus

Take a family-friendly tour of Ephesus. Tailor the tour to keep it engaging for children, focusing on the more fascinating stories and landmarks.

Afternoon: Ephesus Museum

Visit the Ephesus Museum, where kids can see artifacts up close and learn more about ancient history.

Evening: Interactive Dinner

Dine at a restaurant that offers interactive experiences, such as watching the chefs prepare food or live music performances.

Adventure Seeker's Itinerary

Day 1: Arrival and Adventure Prep

Morning: Arrival and Hotel Check-In

Arrive in Kuşadası and check into your adventure base. Choose accommodations that offer easy access to outdoor activities.

Afternoon: Orientation and Gear Check

Get oriented with the town and check your gear for the upcoming adventures. Visit local shops for any last-minute equipment needs.

Evening: Adventure Planning Dinner

Have dinner at a local restaurant while planning your adventure-packed week. Get advice from locals and fellow travelers.

Day 2: Hiking and Exploration

Morning: Dilek Peninsula National Park Hike

Start your adventure with a challenging hike in Dilek Peninsula National Park. Choose a trail that offers both difficulty and scenic views.

Afternoon: Wildlife Spotting

Spend the afternoon wildlife spotting. The park is home to a variety of animals, including wild boar, deer, and numerous bird species.

Evening: Camping or Hotel Return

Depending on your preference, either set up camp in the park (if permitted) or return to your hotel to rest for the next day's activities.

Day 3: Water Adventures

Morning: Scuba Diving

Explore the underwater world with a scuba diving excursion. There are several dive sites around Kuşadası that cater to different skill levels.

Afternoon: Snorkeling and Beach Time

After diving, spend the afternoon snorkeling in the shallow waters. Then relax on the beach and soak up the sun.

Evening: Seafood Dinner by the Sea

Enjoy a seafood dinner at a beachfront restaurant, sharing stories of the day's underwater adventures.

Relaxation and Wellness Itinerary

Day 1: Arrival and Wellness Orientation

Morning: Arrival and Hotel Check-In

Arrive in Kuşadası and check into a wellness retreat or a hotel with spa facilities.

Afternoon: Orientation and Spa Booking

Get oriented with the facilities and book your spa treatments for the week. Take a tour of the wellness center.

Evening: Relaxing Dinner

Enjoy a healthy and relaxing dinner at the hotel's restaurant, focusing on fresh and nutritious options.

Day 2: Spa and Relaxation

Morning: Turkish Bath (Hamam)

Start your wellness journey with a traditional Turkish bath. Enjoy the cleansing rituals and relax in the warm steam.

Afternoon: Massage Therapy

Follow up with a soothing massage therapy session. Choose from various types such as aromatherapy, deep tissue, or hot stone massage.

Evening: Herbal Tea and Meditation

Wind down the day with a session of meditation and a cup of calming herbal tea.

Day 3: Beach and Leisure

Morning: Yoga on the Beach

Participate in a morning yoga session on the beach. The sound of the waves and the gentle sea breeze will enhance your practice.

Afternoon: Beach Relaxation

Spend the afternoon lounging on the beach, reading a book, and swimming in the sea.

Evening: Sunset Walk

Take a peaceful walk along the beach at sunset, enjoying the serene atmosphere.

These itineraries are designed to help you experience the best of Kuşadası, whether you're here for a quick visit or a longer stay. From historical explorations to family fun, adrenaline adventures, and relaxation retreats, there's something for every type of traveler in this beautiful Turkish town. Enjoy your journey and make the most of your time in Kuşadası!

Chapter 8

TRANSPORTATION WITHIN KUŞADASI

Getting about this busy coastal town may be an adventure in itself, complete with the allure of local experiences. Discover Kuşadası's many modes of transportation, each with its own particular character.

Public Transportation: Dolmuş and Buses

The dolmuş captures the character of Kuşadası like no other method of transport. These shared minibuses are more than just transportation; they give a glimpse into local life. The term "dolmuş" literally means "stuffed," and that's how these minibuses often feel, especially during rush hour. But don't let that dissuade you—it's all part of the experience!

Using Dolmuş:

Hopping on a dolmuş is straightforward. They have defined routes but not fixed stops. You can flag one down anywhere along its journey and get off wherever you like. It's a casual system that works surprisingly well. Payment is provided to the driver, and it's a good idea to have some little change on available. A ride costs between 3 and 5 Turkish Lira, making it an affordable option.

Routes and destinations:

Dolmuş routes connect all important areas of Kuşadası, from the busy town center to the quiet beaches. Do you want to visit Ladies Beach? There is a dolmuş for it. Are you planning a vacation to Dilek Peninsula National Park? You can also get there via dolmuş. These minibuses are a wonderful way to view the town from a local's perspective.

Tips for First-time Users:

- **Look for Signs:** Dolmuş routes are usually indicated on signs at the front of the minibus. If in doubt, ask the driver or a local—people are usually very helpful.

- **Be Ready to Stop:** When you want to get off, simply say "inecek var" (someone wants to get off) or press the stop button if available.
- **Peak Times:** Dolmuşes can get congested, particularly during rush hours and during the tourist season. If you aren't in a rush, aim to travel during off-peak hours.

Public buses:

While dolmuşes are the backbone of local transportation, public buses provide a more organized and slightly less congested alternative. They are less frequent, but they cover important routes and are an excellent option if you prefer a little more space.

Using public buses:

Kuşadası Municipality operates public buses. They have specific stops and schedules, which are posted at bus stations and online. Fares are comparable to dolmuşes, and you can pay in cash or with a travel card.

Route and Coverage:

Buses connect the town core with surrounding regions and towns. They are especially essential if you plan to visit nearby locations such as Selçuk or the village of Şirince.

Tips for Bus Travel:

- **Check schedules:** Buses run on a predetermined timetable, so double-check the timings ahead of time.
- **Comfort:** Buses are less congested than dolmuşes and provide a more comfortable journey, particularly over longer distances.

Taxis and Car Rentals

Sometimes, convenience trumps everything else, and that's where taxis and car rentals come into play. Whether you want to go to a destination fast or explore the surrounding areas at your leisure, these options provide flexibility and convenience.

Taxis:

Taxis in Kuşadası are easily identified by their bright yellow color. They are metered, and fares are reasonable by European standards. However, it is always a good idea to have an estimated route to minimize surprises.

Using taxis:

- **Hailing a Taxi:** You can hail a taxi on the street or at authorized taxi stands near popular destinations such as the harbor, bus station, and large hotels.
- **Rates:** The base rate is roughly 5 Turkish Lira, with an extra charge per kilometer. Nightly rates can be slightly higher.
- **Language:** Most cab drivers understand basic English, however having your destination written down or on a map can be useful.

Tips for Taxi Use:

- **Know Your Route:** Use a map app to track your itinerary and confirm the driver is taking the correct path.
- **Agree on Fare for Long Trips:** For longer journeys, like a trip to Ephesus, it's wise to agree on a fare beforehand.

Car Rental:

Renting a car is ideal for people who like independence and the joy of exploring at their own leisure. Kuşadası has several rental firms that offer a variety of vehicles, including compact cars and spacious SUVs.

Renting A Car:

- **Requirements:** You'll need a valid driver's license (an International Driving Permit is recommended), passport, and a credit card.
- **Costs:** Rental fees vary, but expect to spend between 150 and 300 Turkish Lira per day, depending on the car type and season.
- **Fuel:** Fuel is an added cost, and prices are comparable to European levels. Gas stations are widespread and typically take credit cards.

Tips for Car Rental:

- **Book in Advance:** To ensure the greatest rates and availability, book your car ahead of time, especially during peak season.

- **Insurance:** Make sure your rental includes full insurance. It's worth spending a little more for peace of mind.
- **Navigation:** GPS or a reputable map app is required. Road signs are in Turkish, and while major roads are clearly designated, smaller roads might be challenging.

Biking and Walking Routes

Kuşadası's small layout and stunning scenery make it ideal for riding and strolling. There's something for everyone, from casual strollers to experienced cyclists.

Biking:

Renting a bike is an ideal way to explore Kuşadası. Many hotels provide bike rentals, and there are specific rental businesses in town.

Popular Biking Routes:

- **Along the Coast:** The coastline route provides spectacular views of the Aegean Sea. You may

ride from the marina to Ladies Beach and enjoy the fresh sea breeze.
- **Dilek Peninsula:** For the more adventurous, biking to the Dilek Peninsula National Park is a rewarding experience. The park has pathways across lush scenery and stunning views.

Tips for Biking:

- **Safety Gear:** Always wear a helmet and reflective clothing, especially if biking in the evening.
- **Stay Hydrated:** Carry water because it might get hot, especially in the summer.
- **Respect Traffic:** Obey traffic laws and be aware of pedestrians and vehicles.

Walking:

Walking is one of the best ways to experience Kuşadası's charm. The town is pedestrian-friendly, having numerous attractions within walking distance of one another.

Popular walking routes:

- **Old Town:** Wander through the narrow streets of the old town, discovering quaint shops, cafes, and historical sites like the Kaleiçi Mosque.
- **Marina to Pigeon Island**: A walk along the marina provides stunning views of the harbor and leads to Pigeon Island, where you may explore the castle and enjoy panoramic vistas.
- **Ladies Beach Promenade:** The promenade at Ladies Beach is great for an evening walk, with various cafés and restaurants where you can stop for a snack.

Tips for walking:

- **Comfortable Shoes:** Wear comfortable walking shoes, as the cobblestone streets can be uneven.
- **Sun Protection:** Don't forget sunscreen, a hat, and sunglasses, especially in the summertime.
- **Evening Walks:** Walking in the evening is a terrific way to avoid the heat while also enjoying the lively environment as both locals and tourists gather to enjoy the night.

Tips and Tricks for navigating the city

While navigating Kuşadası is simple, there are some helpful tips and methods to maximize your time here.

Maps and navigation apps:

Having a dependable navigation app on your phone is quite useful. While Google Maps works effectively in Kuşadası, offline maps such as Maps.me might serve as a reliable backup.

Street Signs:

Street signs are in Turkish, therefore familiarizing yourself with certain popular terminology like "cadde" (avenue) and "sokak" (street) can be helpful.

Local Tips:

- **Market Haggling:** Haggling is typical when shopping at markets or bazaars. Begin by providing approximately half of the initial price and negotiating from there.
- **Avoiding Crowds:** To avoid the crowds, visit popular attractions early in the morning or later in the afternoon.

- **Local Etiquette:** When visiting religious sites, dress modestly and always ask permission before photographing people.

Emergency Contacts:

It's usually a good idea to keep some emergency contact information available. Here are some important numbers:

- Police: 155
- Ambulance: 112
- Fire Department: 110
- Tourist Police: +90 256 614 63 45

Health and Safety:

- **Water:** Tap water is generally safe for washing but stick to bottled water for drinking.
- **Food:** Street food is delicious but ensure it's from a clean and reputable vendor to avoid any stomach issues.
- **Safety:** Kuşadası is generally safe, but like any tourist destination, keep an eye on your belongings, especially in crowded areas.

In conclusion, getting around Kuşadası is part of the adventure that makes this destination so special. Whether you're mingling with locals on a dolmuş, exploring hidden gems by bike, or simply strolling through the charming streets, every journey is an opportunity to discover something new. So, embrace the local ways, take in the sights, and let the rhythm of Kuşadası guide your travels. Safe travels, and enjoy every moment of your stay in this enchanting coastal town!

Chapter 9

ACCOMMODATION OPTIONS

Choosing the right accommodation in Kuşadası can significantly enhance your holiday experience. Kuşadası offers a variety of rooms to suit any taste and budget. Let's look at the different options that make this seaside jewel such an appealing destination for all types of travelers.

Luxury Resorts and Hotels

Kuşadası delivers exceptional luxury. I've had the privilege of staying in some of the greatest accommodations, and each one is unique.

- **Korumar Hotel De Luxe**

Address: Korumar Hotel De Luxe, Türkmen Mahallesi, Gazi Beğendi Sokak No:13, 09400 Kuşadası, Aydın, Turkey

Perched on a cliff overlooking the Aegean Sea, the Korumar Hotel De Luxe is an excellent choice for visitors seeking a combination of luxury and stunning scenery. The apartments are big and nicely equipped, with balconies offering breathtaking views of the sunset. The hotel's own beach is ideal for a relaxing afternoon, and the infinity pool provides a welcome respite from the sun. Their spa services are exceptional, with a variety of treatments that will leave you feeling invigorated. Dining here is an adventure, with a wide range of restaurants selling everything from traditional Turkish delicacies to foreign cuisine.

- **Charisma de Luxe Hotel**

Address: Charisma De Luxe Hotel, Türkmen Mahallesi, Akyar Mevkii, 09400 Kuşadası, Aydın, Turkey

The Charisma De Luxe Hotel is another outstanding example of opulence. This hotel is renowned for its ultramodern style and superb service. The rooms are created with comfort and style in mind, with floor-to-ceiling windows providing panoramic views of the sea. Another standout feature is the infinity pool, which blends effortlessly into the horizon. The hotel's spa and wellness center is among the best in the area, offering a variety of treatments, including traditional Turkish baths. Dining at Charisma is also a treat, with several restaurants presenting a wide range of cuisines to suit every taste.

- **Aqua Fantasy Aquapark Hotel and Spa.**

Address: Aqua Fantasy Aquapark Hotel & Spa, Pamucak Mevkii, Ephesus Beach, Selçuk, 35920 İzmir, Turkey

For families seeking a luxurious stay with a variety of activities, the Aqua Fantasy Aquapark Hotel & Spa is a wonderful option. This resort is more than a place to stay; it is a destination in and of itself. The rooms are big and family-friendly, with all of the facilities you may require. The Aquapark, one of Turkey's largest, is undoubtedly the highlight. It's a playground for both kids and adults, with tons of slides, pools, and games to enjoy. The resort also provides a variety of food alternatives, including buffet-style restaurants and a la carte dining experiences, ensuring that everyone in the family finds something they enjoy.

Budget-friendly stays

Traveling on a budget should not imply sacrificing comfort or pleasure. Kuşadası provides affordable lodgings with high-quality service and amenities.

- **Ilayda Avantgarde Hotel**

Address: Ilayda Avantgarde Hotel, Atatürk Bulvarı No:42, 09400 Kuşadası, Aydın, Turkey

The Ilayda Avantgarde Hotel is a great example of affordable luxury. This hotel in Kuşadası offers modern, comfortable rooms with spectacular sea views. The rooftop terrace is ideal for breakfast or an evening cocktail, with panoramic views of the town and sea. The staff here is extremely pleasant and helpful, always willing to give recommendations on things to see and do in the neighborhood. The beach, commercial centers, and restaurants are all nearby, making the location ideal for walking around town.

- **Ephesia Hotel**

Address: Ephesia Hotel, Long Beach, 09400 Kuşadası, Aydın, Turkey

If you want a seaside resort on a budget, the Ephesia Hotel is a great option. The accommodations are clean and pleasant, and the hotel's own beach is a terrific place to relax and enjoy the sun. The hotel also features a gorgeous garden and an outdoor pool. The buffet restaurant serves a wide range of dishes, so there's always something great to taste.

The location is little outside of the main town, yet it's ideal for a more tranquil and relaxed stay.

- **Venti Hotel Luxury**

Address: Venti Hotel Luxury, Yılmaz Efendi Sk. No:8, 09400 Kuşadası, Aydın, Turkey

Despite its moniker, Venti Hotel Luxury provides a more affordable choice while maintaining a sense of luxury. The apartments are nicely designed and provide stunning views of the sea or the garden. The hotel has a lovely outdoor pool and a balcony where you can relax with a book or have a drink. The breakfast buffet is extensive, offering a wide range of alternatives to begin your day. The staff are friendly and helpful, making you feel right at home from the time you arrive.

Unique Accommodations: Boutique Hotels and Guesthouses

Kuşadası offers unique lodgings that provide a personalized and private experience.

- **Mr. Happy's – Liman Hotel**

Address: Mr. Happy's – Liman Hotel, Hacifeyzullah Mahallesi, Güvercinada Cd. No:19, 09400 Kuşadası, Aydın, Turkey

One of my personal favorites is Mr. Happy's – Liman Hotel. This beautiful boutique hotel, located near the port, provides stunning views and a welcoming atmosphere. Each room is uniquely furnished with traditional Turkish design elements. The rooftop patio, with its wonderful views of the sea and town, is ideal for breakfast or an evening drink. The owner, Mr. Happy, and his team are extremely warm and eager to provide information about Kuşadası. Staying here seems like visiting old friends, making for an unforgettable experience.

- **Anzac Gold Bed Boutique Pension**

Address: Anzac Golden Bed Boutique Pension, Yıldırım Cad. No:69, 09400 Kuşadası, Aydın, Turkey

If you're seeking for a really unique experience, the Anzac Golden Bed Boutique Pension is an excellent alternative. This guesthouse is housed in a historic building in the old town and provides a look into the past with its traditional architecture and decor. The rooms are comfortable and full of character, each one unique from the others. The pension features a wonderful garden where you may relax and sip

Turkish tea. Mary, the proprietor, is an excellent host who enjoys sharing her knowledge and enthusiasm for Kuşadası. Staying here gives you the feeling of being in the heart of town, with all of the sights and noises just a short walk away.

- **Sezgins Boutique Hotel**

Address: Sezgins Boutique Hotel, Aslanlar Cd. No:44, 09400 Kuşadası, Aydın, Turkey

For individuals who value art and creativity, Sezgins Boutique Hotel is an excellent choice. The hotel is loaded with artwork and one-of-a-kind decor, resulting in a dynamic and artistic atmosphere. The rooms are comfortable, elegant, and equipped with modern conveniences. The garden area is a tranquil hideaway, ideal for unwinding after a day of exploration. The hotel also provides a variety of activities and tours, making it simple to explore the surroundings. Sezgin, the proprietor, is an artist himself and frequently arranges art classes and events, which adds to the interest of your stay.

Choosing the Right Accommodation for You

When planning a trip to Kuşadası, selecting the appropriate lodging is crucial. The type of place you stay can greatly influence your overall experience, so it's worth taking some time to consider your options. Here's a complete guide to help you make the best decision.

- **Consider your budget.**

First and foremost, set your budget. Kuşadası provides a variety of accommodations, including luxury resorts, budget-friendly hotels, and distinctive boutique guesthouses. Knowing how much you can afford to spend will help you reduce your options.

- **Identify your priorities.**

Consider what's most essential to you throughout your visit. Are you seeking for a seaside position, close to the city center, or a peaceful retreat? Do you like a hotel with a pool and spa, or are you looking for a place with local charm and character? Identifying your priorities will allow you to focus on the lodgings that best fit your requirements.

- **Travel companions**

Consider who you're traveling with. If you're traveling as a couple, a romantic boutique hotel could be perfect. For families, a resort featuring kid-friendly activities, such as the Aqua Fantasy Aquapark Hotel & Spa, would be ideal. Solo visitors may prefer a central location, such as the Ilayda Avantgarde Hotel, which provides convenient access to the town's attractions.

- **length of stay**

The length of your visit can also influence your accommodation selection. For longer visits, choose hotels with kitchenettes or serviced flats, which allow you to prepare your own meals and feel more at home.

- **Season and Availability.**

The time of year you travel can influence the availability and cost of accommodations. During peak tourist season, rates tend to rise, and popular hotels may be fully booked. If you travel during the off-season, you may find better prices and greater availability.

Booking Tips and Tricks

Once you've decided on the type of lodging that best meets your needs, it's time to arrange your stay. Here are some tips and methods to help you get the greatest deal and have a smooth booking experience.

- **Book Early**

Booking your accommodation ahead of time is one of the greatest methods to get the best rates and availability. This is especially important if you're traveling during high season or have set your sights on a specific hotel.

- **Be flexible with dates.**

Flexible travel dates can often lead to greater bargains. Check several date ranges to see whether extending your stay by a few days can save you money.

- **Compare prices.**

Compare costs across several booking platforms. Websites such as Booking.com, Expedia, and Agoda frequently offer multiple rates and specials for the same hotel. Don't forget to check the hotel's own website, since they occasionally offer exceptional rates for direct bookings.

- **Read reviews.**

Before you book, check other travelers' reviews. Websites such as TripAdvisor and Google Reviews provide information about previous guests' experiences. Expect consistent reviews on cleanliness, service, and amenities.

- **Look for discounts and promotions.**

Keep an eye out for deals and promotions. Many booking sites and hotels provide special discounts for early bookings, extended stays, and last-minute reservations. You can also get savings through membership programs like AAA, AARP, or frequent flyer programs.

- **Check cancellation policies.**

Before making a booking, be sure you understand the cancellation policy. Some tariffs are non-refundable, while others allow free cancellation until a specified date. A flexible cancellation policy can offer piece of mind if your vacation plans change.

- **Contact the hotel directly.**

If you have any unique requirements or questions, please do not hesitate to contact the hotel directly. They can provide more specific information and may possibly provide a lower rate than what is shown online.

Booking Platforms

There are numerous booking platforms available that can help you find and book the perfect accommodation in Kuşadası. Here are a few of the most popular:

- **Booking.com**

Booking.com is one of the largest and most popular booking sites. It has a diverse range of accommodations, including luxury resorts, budget-friendly hotels, and guesthouses. The platform is user-friendly, with numerous filters to help you find exactly what you're looking for. You may also read other travelers' evaluations and take advantage of regular bargains and promotions.

- **Expedia**

Expedia is another significant booking platform that provides a wide range of lodgings. Expedia not only offers hotels but also flights, car rentals, and excursions, making it a simple one-stop shop for all of your travel needs. The platform frequently offers bundle deals that allow you to save money.

- **Airbnb**

Airbnb is an excellent choice for anyone seeking one-of-a-kind, homey accommodations. Private rooms and communal spaces are available, as well as complete homes and apartments. Airbnb frequently offers a more local experience, allowing you to stay in residential areas and engage with hosts who can provide insider information.

- **Agoda**

Agoda is renowned in Asia and provides accommodations globally, including Kuşadası. The marketplace is well-known for its affordable pricing and frequently offers exclusive discounts. Agoda also has a rewards program in which you may collect points for each booking and redeem them for savings on future stays.

- **Hotels.com**

Hotels.com has a large selection of rooms and a rewards program that allows you to earn one free night for every ten nights booked. The site routinely provides special bargains and discounts, making it an excellent choice for budget-conscious travelers.

- **TripAdvisor**

TripAdvisor is well-known for its vast collection of traveler reviews and ratings. In addition to purchasing hotels, TripAdvisor can help you find restaurants, sights, and tours. The software allows you to compare costs from several booking sites to locate the cheapest deal.

- **Hotel Websites**

Remember to verify the official websites of the hotels you're interested in. Hotels may provide exclusive incentives for direct bookings, such as free upgrades, complementary breakfast, or reduced pricing. Booking directly also allows you additional flexibility with cancellations and specific requests.

In summary, Kuşadası offers a wide range of accommodation options to suit every traveler's needs and preferences. Whether you're seeking for luxury, low-cost accommodations, or one-of-a-kind boutique experiences, you'll find the ideal location to stay. Each of these accommodations provides a different perspective on the town, enhancing your overall experience and making your stay in Kuşadası truly unforgettable.

Chapter 10

DINING AND NIGHTLIFE IN KUŞADASI

Whether you're a foodie looking to sample traditional Turkish dishes, a party-goer seeking a lively atmosphere, or someone who enjoys a quiet evening with a good meal and a view, Kuşadası has something to offer. Let me take you through some of my favorite spots and experiences that make dining and nightlife in Kuşadası truly memorable.

Must-Try Restaurants

- **Kazim Usta Restaurant**

Address: Atatürk Bulvarı No: 94, 09400 Kuşadası, Aydın, Turkey

One of the first places I recommend is Kazim Usta Restaurant. Located by the sea, this restaurant offers an extensive menu that showcases the best of Turkish cuisine. The seafood here is exceptionally fresh, with dishes like grilled octopus and stuffed mussels that will leave you craving more. The atmosphere is relaxed, with the sound of waves gently lapping against the shore, making it a perfect spot for a romantic dinner or a family gathering.

Special Tips:

- Try the grilled seabass – it's cooked to perfection with just the right amount of seasoning.
- Make a reservation if you plan to dine during sunset to enjoy the breathtaking views.

- **Avlu Bistro Bar**

Address: Camikebir Mahallesi, Bozkurt Sk. No: 4, 09400 Kuşadası, Aydın, Turkey

For those who prefer a mix of traditional and contemporary dishes, Avlu Bistro Bar is the place to be. Nestled in the heart of the town, this bistro offers a cozy courtyard setting where you can enjoy dishes like lamb shank, moussaka, and their famous avocado salad. The ambiance here is warm and inviting, making it a great place to unwind after a day of sightseeing.

Special Tips:

- The homemade lemonade is incredibly refreshing and pairs well with their Mediterranean dishes.
- Their desserts, especially the baklava, are not to be missed.

- **Saray Restaurant**

Address: Kaleiçi Mahallesi, Barbaros Hayrettin Paşa Blv. No: 36, 09400 Kuşadası, Aydın, Turkey

Saray Restaurant is another gem that offers a wide range of Turkish and Ottoman cuisine. The interior is elegantly decorated, giving you a sense of dining in a traditional Turkish home. The menu is extensive, with options for vegetarians and meat lovers alike. From kebabs to mezes, every dish is prepared with great attention to detail.

Special Tips:

- Order a variety of mezes to share – it's a fantastic way to sample different flavors.
- Their house-made raki is the perfect way to end your meal.

Street Food Delights

- **Kumpir at the Waterfront**

Address: Along Atatürk Bulvarı, Kuşadası Marina Area, 09400 Kuşadası, Aydın, Turkey

If you're a fan of street food, Kuşadası's waterfront is the place to explore. One of my all-time favorites is kumpir, a Turkish-style baked potato. Vendors along the waterfront fill these giant potatoes with a variety of toppings, from cheese and sausage to olives and corn. It's a quick, delicious, and filling option that you can enjoy while strolling by the sea.

Special Tips:
- Don't be shy to ask for extra toppings – the more, the merrier!
- Pair your kumpir with a cold ayran, a traditional Turkish yogurt drink.

- **Simit from Local Bakeries**

Address: Various bakeries throughout Kuşadası, with popular spots along the main streets and markets.

Another must-try street food is simit, often referred to as the Turkish bagel. These sesame-encrusted bread rings are crispy on the outside and soft on the inside. You'll find simit vendors and local bakeries selling these treats throughout the day.

Special Tips:

- Enjoy simit with a slice of beyaz peynir (white cheese) and a cup of Turkish tea for a traditional breakfast experience.
- They're perfect for a quick snack or a light breakfast on the go.

Best Spots for Nightlife and Entertainment

- **Jade Beach Club**

Address: Türkmen Mahallesi, Atatürk Blv. No: 36, 09400 Kuşadası, Aydın, Turkey

When the sun sets, Kuşadası's nightlife comes alive, and one of the best places to experience it is Jade Beach Club. This beachfront venue transforms into a lively party spot with DJs spinning the latest tunes, themed parties, and live performances. The atmosphere is electric, with locals and tourists mingling and dancing the night away.

Special Tips:

- Arrive early to secure a good spot, especially on weekends when it gets crowded.
- Check their schedule for special events and live music nights.

- **Jimmy's Irish Bar**

Address: Kaleiçi Mahallesi, Kahramanlar Cd. No: 23, 09400 Kuşadası, Aydın, Turkey

For a more laid-back evening, head to Jimmy's Irish Bar. This cozy pub offers a wide selection of beers, spirits, and cocktails, along with a warm and friendly atmosphere. It's a great place to relax, chat with fellow travelers, and enjoy live music.

Special Tips:

- Try their signature cocktails – the bartenders here are quite creative.
- Their live music nights are a hit, so make sure to catch a performance if you can.

- **Orient Bar**

Address: Türkmen Mahallesi, Atatürk Blv. No: 46, 09400 Kuşadası, Aydın, Turkey

If you're in the mood for something different, the Orient Bar is a must-visit. This rooftop bar offers stunning views of Kuşadası and the Aegean Sea. The decor is chic, and the vibe is sophisticated, making it an ideal spot for a more upscale evening out. Sip on expertly crafted cocktails while watching the sunset, and stay for the lively atmosphere that continues into the night.

Special Tips:
- The mojitos here are exceptional – highly recommended!
- It's a great place for a date night or a special occasion.

Wine Tasting and Local Brews

- **Sevilen Winery**

Address: Şirince Köyü Yolu, 35920 Selçuk, İzmir, Turkey (a short drive from Kuşadası)

Kuşadası is not just about beaches and nightlife; it's also a great place to explore local wines. A visit to Sevilen Winery offers a delightful experience of wine tasting amidst beautiful vineyards. The winery produces a range of wines that reflect the unique terroir of the region.

Special Tips:

- Take a guided tour to learn about the winemaking process and the history of the winery.
- Sample a variety of wines to find your favorite – their whites are particularly refreshing.

- **Kusadasi Brewery**

Address: Yavansu Mahallesi, Karaova Sk. No: 5, 09400 Kuşadası, Aydın, Turkey

For beer enthusiasts, a visit to Kusadasi Brewery is a must. This local brewery offers a selection of craft beers that are brewed with passion and expertise. From pale ales to stouts, there's something to suit every palate.

Special Tips:

- The brewery tour is informative and includes tastings of their best brews.
- Don't leave without trying their seasonal specials – they're always a pleasant surprise.

Conclusion

Dining and nightlife in Kuşadası offer a vibrant mix of experiences that cater to all tastes and preferences. Whether you're savoring traditional Turkish dishes, enjoying a casual street food snack, dancing the night away at a beach club, or relaxing with a glass of local wine, there's always something new and exciting to discover. My time in Kuşadası has been filled with memorable meals and unforgettable nights, and I'm confident that you'll find your own favorite spots and experiences in this beautiful town.

Chapter 11

SHOPPING IN KUŞADASI

Kuşadası offers a delightful shopping experience for all travelers. There's something for everyone, from busy bazaars full of colorful textiles to sophisticated malls stocked with worldwide brands. Kuşadası offers a variety of attractions, including unique souvenirs, local crafts, and a lively environment. Allow me to guide you through some of the best shopping experiences this quaint Turkish town has to offer.

Best Shopping Streets and Malls

Bar Street

Bar Street is not just famous for its nightlife; it's also a great spot for shopping. By day, this street transforms into a bustling market where you can discover a wide range of things. The stalls here sell a wide range of products, from fashionable clothing and accessories to handcrafted items. The merchants are pleasant and often willing to bargain costs, providing for an enjoyable and interesting buying experience.

Scala Nuova Shopping Center

Scala Nuova Shopping Center, located near the cruise terminal, is an ideal destination for those arriving by boat. This sophisticated shopping mall features a mix of local and international brands, catering to a diverse range of tastes and budgets. It's an excellent spot to get last-minute necessities or discover a unique gift for loved ones back home. There are also various cafes and restaurants in the center, where you may relax and eat.

Grand Bazaar

The Grand Bazaar is a must-see on any journey to Kuşadası. This vast bazaar is a sensory overload in the greatest way. The small alleys are dotted with stores that sell everything from spices and sweets to leather items and jewellery. The brilliant colors, tantalizing smells, and energetic banter of merchants make for a unique shopping experience. Prepare to haggle, as negotiating is common and may be rather pleasant.

Kaleiçi

Kaleiçi, the old town of Kuşadası, is a tangle of picturesque streets and lanes, each filled with stores offering a range of products. Traditional Turkish carpets and linens are available here, as well as unusual antiques and antiquities. The historic location adds to the appeal, making it an ideal spot for wandering, shopping, and taking in the ambiance.

Novada Outlet Söke.

For those who enjoy a good bargain, the Novada Outlet Söke is a must-see. This outlet mall, a short drive from Kuşadası, offers discounts on a variety of local and international products. It's an excellent site to get high-quality things at low rates, including clothes, accessories, home goods, and electronics.

Souvenirs to Take Home

Bringing home a slice of Kuşadası is a terrific way to remember the trip and share it with friends and family. Here are some of the top souvenirs to consider:

Turkish Carpets and Kilims

Turkish carpets and kilims are known for their beautiful designs and craftsmanship. Whether you choose a tiny ornamental rug or a bigger piece, these textiles make lovely and practical mementos. Shops in Kuşadası provide a diverse assortment and allow visitors to observe craftspeople at work, enhancing their appreciation for these pieces of art.

Iznik Ceramics

Iznik ceramics are known for their brilliant colors and elaborate designs. These lovely pieces come in a variety of shapes, including plates, bowls, tiles, and vases. Each piece is a work of art, making it an ideal present or a magnificent addition to any home decor.

Olive Oil Products

The Kuşadası region is noted for its olive fields and high-quality olive oil products. Bottles of pure olive oil, soaps, and skincare goods make excellent mementos that capture the character of the place.

Turkish Delight

Turkish delight, also known as "lokum," is a sweet dessert that has been savored for centuries. It's a tasty and portable keepsake that comes in a variety of flavors and is frequently elegantly wrapped. Many shops provide free samples, allowing you to taste before you buy.

Handicrafts and Textiles

Kuşadası is home to many skilled artisans, and you can find a wide range of handcrafted items. Look for handmade linens, embroidered tablecloths, and other stunning objects that demonstrate traditional Turkish craftsmanship. These things not only make interesting keepsakes, but they also benefit local artists.

Local Artisans & Crafts

Discovering the local arts and crafts sector in Kuşadası is a fulfilling experience. A diverse group of brilliant craftspeople creates gorgeous, one-of-a-kind objects that reflect the region's rich cultural heritage.

Carpet Weaving

Carpet weaving is a traditional craft that has been passed down through the generations. Visit Kuşadası workshops to witness experienced weavers at work. Many of these artists utilize natural dyes and traditional techniques to make beautiful carpets and kilims. It's a fascinating process to watch, and you'll have a greater understanding for the time and talent required.

Pottery and Ceramics

Pottery and ceramics are another prominent Turkish tradition. Kuşadası boasts workshops and studios where artisans use centuries-old techniques to make stunning creations. Whether you're looking for useful goods like bowls and plates or ornamental pieces, you'll discover plenty of choices.

Jewelry Making

Kuşadası is known for its beautiful handmade jewelry. The jewelry on display here is one-of-a-kind, with exquisite silver pieces and gorgeous jewels that often mimic traditional Turkish motifs. Many businesses provide custom-made items, allowing you to take home a genuinely unique keepsake.

Practical Tips for Shopping in Kuşadası

To maximize your shopping experience in Kuşadası, consider the following tips:

- **Haggle with Confidence:** Bargaining is common in many markets and stores. Begin by offering a lesser price than you are willing to pay, and enjoy the negotiation process with the vendor.
- **Check for Authenticity:** When purchasing products such as rugs, porcelain, and jewelry, ensure their authenticity. High-value products are frequently accompanied with certifications of authenticity from reputable merchants.
- **Carry Cash:** While many businesses take credit cards, smaller shops and market booths frequently prefer cash. Carrying some local cash is a smart idea for smaller purchases and haggling.
- **Pack Smart:** If you intend to purchase larger items such as rugs or pottery, consider how you will bring them home. Many stores provide shipping services, but it is necessary to compare prices and delivery timeframes.
- **Stay Hydrated:** Shopping in the busy marketplaces and streets of Kuşadası can be

exhausting. Drink plenty of water, particularly during the hot summer months.

Shopping in Kuşadası offers more than just souvenirs; it's a chance to connect with local artisans and immerse yourself in their culture. Whether visiting the vibrant bazaars or exploring modest artisan workshops, each shopping trip is an opportunity to discover something new and take a piece of Kuşadası home.

Chapter 12

WHAT TO DO AND NOT TO DO IN KUŞADASI

Having spent a significant amount of time meandering through its lovely alleyways, delighting in local cuisines, and immersing myself in the dynamic culture, I can tell you that there are a few must-dos and don'ts that will help you make the most of your stay while respecting local customs and traditions. Let's go into the details!

Important Dos and Don'ts for Tourists

Do embrace the local culture.

Kuşadası is a blend of ancient and modern, preserving traditional values. One of the most effective ways to connect with a place is to embrace its culture. Attend local festivals, converse with people, and sample traditional Turkish tea. People here are exceedingly kind and willing to share their culture with guests.

Don't ignore dress codes.

Although Kuşadası is a popular tourist destination with a carefree attitude, it is recommended to dress modestly when visiting religious sites or traditional neighborhoods. Women should cover their shoulders and knees, while men should avoid wearing shorts in certain areas. This regard for local norms goes a long way toward having a positive encounter.

Do try local cuisine.

Kuşadası provides a diverse selection of Turkish food to satisfy all senses. Don't pass up trying local specialties including as kebabs, mezes, and baklava. For an authentic experience, visit local restaurants and street food booths. You will not regret it, believe me!

Don't stick to International Chains

While it's tempting to stick with established multinational food franchises, venturing out of your comfort zone and visiting local restaurants will provide a more enriching experience. The flavors, ambiance, and encounters you will have in these establishments are unparalleled.

Do bargain at bazaars.

Bargaining is a typical occurrence in Turkish markets and bazaars. It's expected and can be rather enjoyable! When shopping for souvenirs, spices, or textiles, feel free to haggle, but do it with a smile and courtesy. It's part of the local shopping culture, which enhances the experience.

Don't acept the First Price

Vendors frequently start with a higher price, expecting you to bargain. Negotiate politely and seek a compromise. Remember that, while negotiating is part of the culture, being fair and respectful is essential.

Do carry cash.

While credit cards are generally accepted in many areas, smaller stores, marketplaces, and local restaurants may prefer cash. Carrying some Turkish Lira with you will make transactions go more smoothly and prevent any inconvenience.

Do use local transportation.

Navigating Kuşadası is an adventure in itself. Local dolmuş (minibuses) provide an economical and efficient mode of transportation. They are more than just a mode of transportation; they provide an experience that allows you to explore the city through the eyes of a native.

Cultural Sensitivities and Respectful Behavior

Respect for Religion

Turkey is largely Muslim, thus honoring religious rituals is crucial. During prayer times, mosques may issue a call to prayer. It's a beautiful, melancholy sound that is an essential part of everyday living. When visiting mosques, dress modestly, remove your shoes before entering, and remain silent out of respect.

Greetings and Social Etiquette

A pleasant hello in Turkish can go a long way. "Merhaba" means "hello," whereas "Teşekkür ederim" means "thank you." Learning a few fundamental phrases can make conversations more interesting. Turks are often quite friendly and welcoming. When welcomed to someone's home, it's usual to offer a small present, such as candy or flowers.

Photography Etiquette:

When photographing Kuşadası, it's important to obtain permission, especially in traditional or religious settings. Some areas may have photography limits, therefore it's important to be aware of and observe those rules.

Environmental Respect

Kuşadası's natural beauty is one of its main attractions. As a responsible tourist, you can help keep things that way. When visiting nature reserves or historical places, avoid littering, bring reusable water bottles, and adhere to the requirements. Respect wildlife and natural ecosystems to help protect the environment for future generations.

Safety Tips and Common Scams to Avoid

Personal Safety

Although Kuşadası is generally safe, as with any tourist attraction, it's important to exercise caution. Keep a watch on your belongings, particularly in crowded areas. Use hotel safes to store your valuables, and use caution while taking money from ATMs.

Taxi scams

While most taxi drivers are honest, there have been isolated reports of scams. When you begin your ride, make sure the meter is running, and if you are uncomfortable, don't be afraid to urge the driver to stop and get out. Pre-arranging transfers through your hotel may also be a safer choice.

Street vendors and tours.

Be wary of aggressive street merchants and unwanted offers for excursions. It is advisable to schedule tours through trustworthy providers or at your hotel. If something feels strange, follow your instincts and walk away.

Health precautions

Carry a basic first-aid kit, including any personal prescriptions. To ensure safety, avoid drinking tap water in Kuşadası and instead opt for bottled water. It is also a good idea to obtain travel insurance that covers health and emergency.

Emergency Contacts:

Familiarize oneself with local emergency numbers. The universal emergency number in Turkey is 112, which includes police, fire, and medical services. It is also helpful to have the contact information for your embassy or consulate in case you require assistance.

To ensure an enjoyable and polite visit to Kusadası, follow these dos and don'ts. Accept the local culture, enjoy the cuisine, and immerse yourself in the rich history and natural beauty. Respecting local customs and being aware of your surroundings can not only improve your experience but also have a good impact on this wonderful location.

Chapter 13

PRACTICAL INFORMATION

Welcome to the practical side of your journey to Kuşadası! Having spent considerable time exploring this gem on the Aegean coast, I've gathered all the essential information you'll need to make your visit smooth and enjoyable. This chapter covers everything from currency and communication to health and safety tips. So, let's dive in and get you well-prepared for your adventure.

Currency and Money Exchange

When arriving in Kuşadası, it's important to first organize your finances. The Turkish Lira (TRY) is the official currency locally. I found it convenient to convert my money at the airport, although this may also be done in banks, exchange offices (Döviz), and even some hotels. Rates are usually competitive, but it's always a good idea to shop around for the best offer.

ATMs are readily available, and the majority of them accept international cards. I always carried some cash, especially for modest transactions or for visiting more remote places. While credit and debit cards are widely accepted in Kuşadası's hotels, restaurants, and shops, local markets and smaller eateries prefer cash.

Tips for Currency Exchange:

- Check the conversion rate before leaving, and compare rates at several exchange offices.
- Except in an emergency, avoid exchanging money at your hotel; the rates may be less beneficial.
- Always notify your bank of your vacation plans to avoid any card complications while overseas.

Language & Communication

Turkish is the official language of Kuşadası. While many individuals in tourist destinations understand English, particularly those in the hospitality business, learning a few basic Turkish words can be extremely beneficial. Locals appreciate the effort, which might improve your experience.

When I first arrived, I had a translation app with me, which came in handy in more remote regions where English was not widely spoken. Kuşadası has decent mobile connectivity and offers easy access to local SIM cards for internet and calls. Major providers such as Turkcell, Vodafone, and Türk Telekom give a variety of packages.

Health and Safety Tips

Staying healthy and safe is essential on any journey. While Kuşadası is generally a safe tourist site, it's important to exercise caution.

Health Tips:

- Drink bottled water. Tap water is normally acceptable for brushing teeth and taking a shower, but bottled water is preferred for drinking.
- Pack a basic first aid pack that includes pain killers, band-aids, and any prescription medications you may require.
- Pharmacies (Eczane) are widespread, and pharmacists can assist with minor diseases. They

frequently speak English and can dispense over-the-counter drugs.

Safety Tips:

- Always keep a watch on your valuables, especially in congested areas such as marketplaces and public transportation.
- Use a trustworthy cab service or ridesharing app. If you rent a car, park in well-lit and secure areas.
- Stay up to date on any travel advisories or local news, especially if you plan excursions outside of the main tourist sites.

Staying connected

It is critical to stay in touch with loved ones and have access to information while traveling. As previously stated, cellphone connectivity is generally good. Here's some more information on staying connected:

SIM Cards & Mobile Data:

- **Turkcell:** Known for wide coverage and good data packages.

- Vodafone: Provides affordable pricing and dependable service.
- **Türk Telekom:** Another solid choice with a variety of bundles.

SIM cards can be purchased at the airport, mobile stores, and kiosks across the city. When acquiring a SIM card, you will need to show your passport.

Internet Access:

- **Wi-Fi:** Most hotels, cafes, and restaurants offer free Wi-Fi. It's usually fast enough for basic browsing and video calls.
- **Portable WiFi Devices:** If you need reliable internet while on the go, try renting a portable Wi-Fi gadget. These can be booked online and picked up at the airport or delivered to your hotel.

Navigating Public Services

Understanding how to use public services can help you save time and effort. This is a quick guide:

Postal Services:

- **Post Offices:** Look for the yellow PTT signs. They provide mailing services, bill payments, and currency conversion.
- **Sending Postcards:** Stamps can be purchased at PTT offices or souvenir shops. Place your postcards in the yellow PTT mailboxes.

Banking Services:

- **Banks:** Open from Monday to Friday, typically 9 AM to 5 PM. They provide money exchange, ATM services, and more.
- **ATMs:** Widely available and often offer instructions in multiple languages.

Laundry Services:

- **Hotels:** Most hotels offer laundry services, but they can be pricey.
- **Local Laundries:** Look for "Kuru Temizleme" (dry cleaning) signs. They frequently provide washing and ironing services at inexpensive rates.

Environmental Awareness

As a responsible traveler, you should be aware of your environmental impact. Maintaining the natural beauty of Kuşadası is vital.

Sustainable practices:

- **Reduce Plastic Use:** Carry a reusable water bottle and shopping bag.
- **Support Local Businesses:** Choose local items and services to help the local economy and lower your carbon impact.
- **Respect Nature:** Stick to established routes in natural parks, don't trash, and be respectful of the wildlife.
- **Recycling:** Recycling bins are available in many public areas. Separate your waste properly, and encourage others to do the same.

Kuşadası offers something for everyone. Whether you come for the history, the beaches, or the rich culture, you will have a memorable time. Remember to take lots of photos, enjoy every moment, and, most importantly, have fun!

CONCLUSION

As my voyage through Kuşadası concludes, I am left with a kaleidoscope of memories to cherish forever. This charming coastal town in Turkey has a way of capturing your heart and soul, leaving you wanting more. Let me take you through a complete reflection on the highlights of this enchanting site, share final advice for a good visit, and encourage you to return and explore more of what Kuşadası has to offer.

Final Tips for an Enjoyable Visit

- Embrace the Local Culture
- Stay Hydrated and Sun-Protected
- Plan Your Itinerary Wisely
- Use Public Transportation
- Respect the Environment

Encouragement to Return and Explore More

As I bid farewell to Kuşadası, I can't help but feel a sense of longing to return. This charming village has a way of leaving an indelible impression, and there's always something new to uncover. Kuşadası welcomes visitors to revisit their favorite sites or discover hidden gems they overlooked during their first visit.

Kuşadası is more than just a place, but an unforgettable experience. The warmth of its people, the richness of its history, and the beauty of its surroundings combine to produce a one-of-a-kind blend that is difficult to replicate anywhere. When planning your next adventure, consider returning to Kuşadası. There is always more to see, experience, and fall in love with.

In conclusion, Kuşadası is a treasure trove of wonders waiting to be explored. From historic ruins and gorgeous beaches to vibrant culture and natural beauty, this town has a story to tell. Whether you're a first-time or returning tourist, Kuşadası offers a memorable voyage full of adventure, relaxation, and discovery. Prepare to be enchanted by Kuşadası.

APPENDIX: USEFUL RESOURCES

Emergency Contacts

Having access to emergency contacts is crucial when traveling. Here are the important numbers and services you should keep handy while in Kuşadası:

General Emergency (Police, Fire, Medical)

- Emergency Number: 112
- Police Department
- Local Police Station: +90 256 614 10 10
- Tourist Police: +90 256 614 32 32

Fire Department

- Local Fire Station: +90 256 614 11 11

Medical Services

- Kuşadası State Hospital: +90 256 614 15 15
- Private Kuşadası Hospital: +90 256 612 72 72
- Ambulance Service: 112

Embassy Contacts

- US Embassy (Ankara): +90 312 455 55 55
- UK Embassy (Ankara): +90 312 455 33 44
- Canadian Embassy (Ankara): +90 312 409 27 00

Coast Guard

- Coast Guard Command Center: 158

Maps and Navigational Tools

Navigating Kuşadası is easier with the right tools. Here are some maps and navigational aids to help you find your way:

City Maps

- **Tourist Information Centers:** Pick up a free city map at any tourist information center in Kuşadası.
- **Hotel Lobbies:** Many hotels provide complimentary maps of the area.

Online Maps and Apps

- **Google Maps:** Comprehensive and reliable for navigating streets, finding attractions, and planning routes.
- **Maps.me:** An offline map app, which is particularly useful if you don't have access to the internet.
- **Citymapper:** Great for public transportation routes and schedules.

Local Maps

- **Printed Maps:** Available at bookstores, kiosks, and tourist shops. These often include detailed maps of specific attractions like Ephesus and Dilek Peninsula National Park.

Additional Reading and References

To enrich your understanding of Kuşadası and its surrounding areas, consider diving into these additional reading materials and references:

Books

- **"Turkey: Bright Sun, Strong Tea" by Tom Brosnahan** - A humorous and insightful travelogue that captures the essence of traveling through Turkey.

- **"A Traveller's History of Turkey" by Richard Stoneman** - An excellent resource for history buffs who want to understand the deep historical context of their travels.
- **"The Rough Guide to Turkey**" - Comprehensive guidebook with detailed information about Kuşadası and other Turkish destinations.

Websites

- **Turkey Tourism (www.goturkey.com)** - The official tourism portal of Turkey with valuable information and travel tips.
- **TripAdvisor (www.tripadvisor.com)** - User reviews and recommendations for hotels, restaurants, and attractions in Kuşadası.
- **Lonely Planet (www.lonelyplanet.com)** - Travel guides and blogs with practical tips and insights.

Articles and Blogs

Travel blogs often provide personal experiences and tips that can be very helpful. Look for blogs by seasoned travelers who have explored Kuşadası in depth.

Online travel magazines like National Geographic Traveler and Condé Nast Traveler also offer articles on Turkish destinations.

Useful Local Phrases

Learning a few basic phrases in Turkish can enhance your travel experience and help you connect with locals. Here are some useful phrases to get you started:

Greetings and Basic Conversation

- Hello: Merhaba
- Good morning: Günaydın
- Good evening: İyi akşamlar
- Goodbye: Hoşça kal (informal) / Güle güle (formal)
- Please: Lütfen
- Thank you: Teşekkür ederim
- You're welcome: Rica ederim
- Yes: Evet
- No: Hayır
- Excuse me/Sorry: Affedersiniz
- How are you?: Nasılsınız? (formal) / Nasılsın? (informal)

- I am fine, thank you: İyiyim, teşekkür ederim

Directions and Transportation

- Where is...?: ...nerede?
- How much does it cost?: Ne kadar?
- Bus stop: Otobüs durağı
- Train station: Tren istasyonu
- Airport: Havaalanı
- Left: Sol
- Right: Sağ
- Straight ahead: Dümdüz

Dining and Shopping

- Menu: Menü
- Water: Su
- Coffee: Kahve
- Tea: Çay
- How much is this?: Bu ne kadar?
- Check, please: Hesap lütfen
- Delicious: Lezzetli
- Vegetarian: Vejetaryen
- Do you have vegetarian options?: Vejetaryen seçenekleriniz var mı?

Emergencies

- Help!: Yardım!
- I need a doctor: Doktora ihtiyacım var
- Call the police: Polisi arayın
- I'm lost: Kayboldum
- I'm sick: Hastayım

Having these resources at your fingertips will ensure that your time in Kuşadası is as smooth and enjoyable as possible. Safe travels and happy exploring!

MAPS

SCAN HERE TO GAIN DIRECT ACCESS TO THE MAP

https://maps.app.goo.gl/2p6LT8whLtQ8M5ao9

Things to do:
https://maps.app.goo.gl/TS4nCM2JWfgufxtu5

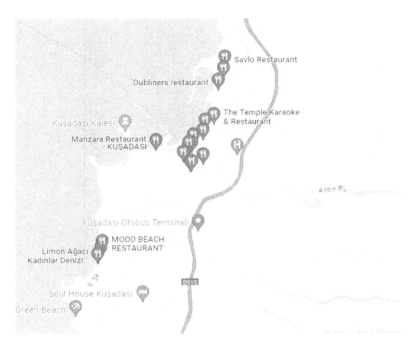

Restaurants:
https://maps.app.goo.gl/9ZbcbGToStY2Q1689

Museums:
https://maps.app.goo.gl/u2VEPRnSGTTWKoKM7

Printed in Great Britain
by Amazon